CONSIDER
One Another

Gospel Advocate®

CONSIDER
One Another

God's Answer to Incivility

AUBREY JOHNSON

Also by Aubrey Johnson

The Barnabas Factor

The Seed Principle

Love More, Sin Less

God's Game Plan

Renewing Your Spiritual Life

The Best Husband Ever

Spiritual Patriots

Music Matters

Dynamic Deacons

The Deacon's Wife

Aubrey's Seminars

Dynamic Deacons

Successful Shepherds

Get Fit! Church Growth through Church Health

The Best Marriage Ever

Published by Gospel Advocate®
1006 Elm Hill Pike, Nashville, TN 37210
www.gospeladvocate.com

ISBN 10: 0-89225-706-7
ISBN 13: 978-0-89225-706-5

This book is dedicated to

Cecil May Jr.

I was invited by Dr. Cecil May Jr. to speak on the topic "Consider One Another" at the Faulkner University Lectures in Montgomery, Alabama. From that assignment came this book. Cecil is one of the most gracious people I have ever known, and I am indebted to him for his friendship and inspiring example of civility.

Special thanks to my friends who helped with this project:

Savannah Cottrell
Lisa Johnson
Lonnie Jones
Dr. John McLaughlin
Dr. Matthew Morine

And let us consider one another in order
to stir up love and good works.

—Hebrews 10:24

Contents

Preface

Being considerate of others will take your children
further in life than any college degree.

—Marian Wright Edelman

This book is a plea for civility and kindness in our troubled times. Imagine the benefits of common courtesy to your family, God's family, and the human family as a whole. What is the secret? More thoughtfulness. Just consider one another. This mental shift accounts for a remarkable increase in satisfying relationships. Considerateness is a basic Christian skill that anyone can learn and practice.

The word "incivility" comes from the Latin *incivilis*, which means "not of a citizen." From a Christian perspective, incivility is behavior unbecoming of a citizen of heaven (Philippians 3:20). Rudeness has no place in the lives of the redeemed. Instead, Christians demonstrate their citizenship in God's kingdom by their high regard for fellow human beings.

George Washington said, "Every action done in company, ought to be with some sign of respect, to those that are present." In other words, concern for others ought to be evident in everything you say and do. Unfortunately, a declining number of people subscribe to this rule. Washington understood that everyone suffers when selfishness rules the day. Without civility, there can be no civilization.

Incivility is not just a problem for society but for churches and families as well. It will take diligent teaching and deliberate practice to reverse the tide. Without courtesy, people become callous and cruel. They lose access to the higher, spiritual functions of the brain. When the capacities for empathy and kindness are diminished, flesh overtakes spirit, and sin vanquishes the soul. The good news is Jesus came to reverse the conscience-deadening effects of sin so that love can reign triumphant in your heart and home.

This book takes a single principle, the command to "consider one another," and demonstrates thirteen ways you can apply it in your daily life. Consideration makes you kind and courteous to everyone. Around strangers, it makes you friendly and hospitable. With family members, you become more faithful and responsible. When trouble comes, consideration helps you to be understanding and forgiving. When differences arise, it makes you reasonable and merciful.

What do these exceptional qualities have in common? They all spring from living thoughtfully rather than reactively. When mindfulness merges with otherness, you are walking by the Spirit rather than the flesh. When tempted or tested, you pause to reflect on the best possible response. Considerateness is mastering the moment of decision for God's glory. It is training your mind to think spiritually rather than selfishly.

There are many ways to put this book to work in your life: read it with your spouse, use it in family devotionals, or study it in a Bible class to spark discussion and deepen your fellowship. Or you could use it for personal study and experiment with the principles Jesus provided for living effectively and abundantly.

However you use this book, my hope is that it will help you and those you love change from the inside out (Romans 12:2). A holy and fruitful life awaits those who practice heaven's rules for healthy relationships. Imagine how enjoyable life will be when you consider one another.

CHAPTER 1
Be Considerate

That best portion of a good man's life, his little, nameless,
unremembered, acts of kindness and of love.

—William Wordsworth

Something is wrong. You sense it in public settings, including the workplace. The divorce rate and misery rate of married couples are proof of the problem. Disrespect, irresponsibility, and lack of self-control are increasing. This decline in civility has resulted in a decay of meaningful relationships and a dramatic drop in the enjoyment of public life. The sense of a coarsening of society has produced feelings of uneasiness everywhere. The problem is obvious, but what can be done about it? Do not despair. God has an answer.

One benefit of Christianity is believers can respond quickly and confidently to social ills. Communities have trouble agreeing on standards or the need for them, but the church has a sure foundation for improving social skills: the teachings of Jesus. Christ declared,

> Therefore whoever hears these sayings of Mine, and does them, I will liken him to a wise man who built his house on the rock: and the rain descended, the floods came, and the winds blew and beat on that house; and it did not fall, for it was founded on the rock. (Matthew 7:24-25)

A wise man is someone who considers the consequences of his choices. He thinks ahead and carefully weighs his options before he speaks or acts. He follows a decision-making protocol that makes outcomes predictable. What is God's will? What are your needs? What is my responsibility? A foolish man is less discerning and disciplined. He is caught up in the moment with little regard for the Father, the future, or the feelings of others. He is more calculating than kind.

The principles taught by Jesus are sure guides to pleasing God and better living. Christians are drawn to these truths by the beauty of the Lord's life. Disciples of Christ devote themselves to becoming more like Jesus in all of their relationships. Rather than sacrificing your identity, following Him refines your distinctive personality to bring out the best in you. Consequently, citizens of heaven make the best citizens on earth. Life is simplified and improved by embracing the eternally relevant teachings of Jesus, and those lessons never become obsolete regardless of societal changes.

THE KEY TO LOVE

According to Jesus, the key to successful living is how you treat other people. In the Sermon on the Mount, He provided heaven's number one rule for healthy relationships: "Therefore, whatever you want men to do to you, do also to them, for this is the Law and the Prophets" (Matthew 7:12). The Golden Rule declares that the basic skill behind Christian living is empathy.

Parents help children cultivate this attitude in the home. Teachers help students develop this outlook in the school. Ministers help members adopt this mindset in the church. This 2,000-year-old rule is the remedy for countless problems, but how do you increase empathy on the earth? One thoughtful person at a time.

The prophet Nathan used questions to awaken David's conscience and help him face the wrong he committed against his servant Uriah. Jesus used questions to help fellow Jews realize the Samaritans they despised were actually their neighbors. Thought-provoking questions help people sense the needs and feelings of others.

A wise mom asks, "How would you like it if someone did that to you?" A discerning dad asks, "What would you want if you were in his situation?" Learning to project yourself into another's circumstances takes effort and practice. The imagination is a tool that can be used for good or evil (Genesis 6:5). Christians train their minds to consider ways to do good and increase joy in the world. Imagination and anticipation are powerful tools for Christian living.

The significance of sympathy was emphasized by Jesus in His depiction of the final judgment.

> When the Son of Man comes in His glory, and all the holy angels with Him, then He will sit on the throne of His glory. All the nations will be gathered before Him, and He will separate them one from another, as a shepherd divides his sheep from the goats. And He will set the sheep on His right hand, but the goats on the left. Then the King will say to those on His right hand, "Come, you blessed of My Father, inherit the kingdom prepared for you from the foundation of the world: for I was hungry and you gave Me food; I was thirsty and you gave Me drink; I was a stranger and you took Me in; I was naked and you clothed Me; I was sick and you visited Me; I was in prison and you came to Me." (Matthew 25:31-36)

Your destiny will be decided by your decency. Human kindness is not the only factor in judgment, but acts of compassion are of great importance to God. Salvation is not based on amassing good works to impress the Lord, but your treatment of others clearly has a bearing on your eternal home. To a large extent, success in life is measured relationally.

THE LANGUAGE OF LOVE

The world uses the word "civility" to describe proper treatment of fellow human beings. Civility is a formal politeness rooted in social convention (common courtesy). The church calls this "consideration" (these terms will be used interchangeably). To consider something is to think about it carefully: to meditate and evaluate. A considerate person anticipates the impact of his actions on others. The goal is not merely sympathy but service. He ponders how to avoid harming or inconveniencing people, but he also contemplates how to relieve or show regard for them.

Paul instructed Christians to think of one another as they go about their daily activities:

> Let nothing be done through selfish ambition or conceit, but in lowliness of mind let each esteem others better than himself. Let each of you look out not only for his own interests, but also for the interests of others. (Philippians 2:3-4)

Spiritually healthy people balance appropriate concern for self with concern for others (Mark 10:31). People who are spiritually unhealthy seldom rise above themselves. The uncivil person is obsessed with his own importance and his own interests. Loving your neighbor as yourself is the way of Christ.

Civility is based on social convention. Consideration is rooted in spiritual transformation. An evil person may be polite but not truly considerate. One is promoted by self-interest (egotism), and the other by mutual interest (empathy). When I think of you and care for you, my actions are sincere. When I treat you well because I am concerned about my image and reputation, my actions are self-serving.

THE SOURCE OF LOVE

Ralph Waldo Emerson said, "[Good manners] ... must be inspired by the good heart." Jesus put it like this: "Every healthy tree bears good fruit, but the diseased tree bears bad fruit" (Matthew 7:17 ESV). The hidden source of a person's words and deeds is the heart from which they spring (Luke 6:45; James 3:11). "You will recognize them by their fruits" (Matthew 7:20 ESV).

Emerson added, "There is no beautifier of ... behavior, like the wish to scatter joy and not pain around us." This observation corresponds to Paul's description of goodness as a fruit of the Spirit. The more your heart is influenced by the teachings of God's Spirit, the more goodness you radiate. You bless rather than burden people and relieve their pressures rather than increase them (Galatians 6:2). It is unhealthy to make a habit of doing for others what they need to do for themselves, but it is wonderful to assist them in handling life's load when they need help. Paul urged, "Do good to all, especially to those who are of the household of faith" (Galatians 6:10b). A life of goodness is the goal of every follower of Christ.

In contrast, evil increases the world's misery. The peculiar thing is that an evil person works hard to justify his heartlessness in his own mind. This is essential to maintain his fragile self-esteem, built upon layers of self-deception. In his mind, you deserved what you got if harm was inflicted, or you were unworthy of help if assistance was withheld. The real truth is he has become very good at rationalizing his selfishness. It is easier to fabricate a lie about you than to face the truth about himself. Therefore, if he must choose, he elects you to be the bad person, and it is no trouble to manufacture the needed evidence with a little practice.

When evil prevails, the usual culprit is a lack of empathy. When good triumphs, the likely explanation is consideration. Thoughtful people seek to relieve suffering and spread joy. Paul wrote, "And be kind to one another, tenderhearted, forgiving one another, even as God in Christ forgave you" (Ephesians 4:32). The apostle understood that kind actions spring from tender hearts. The greatest kindness is to forgive, but other acts of love are presented in the preceding verses. Honesty, patience, generosity, and encouraging words are gracious gifts that arise from a redeemed heart (vv. 25-31). Lying, angry outbursts, stealing, and slander are signs of a heart that is past feeling (vv. 17-19). The central issue in both cases is the condition of the heart.

THE BENEFITS OF LOVE

The benefits of a caring life are self-evident. Without civility, life is disappointing if not disturbing. With kindness, it is not only bearable but beautiful. The wonderful thing is that God allows you to choose how you will live, but rest assured, He will also let you experience the consequences of your decision. Will you be respectful or rude, disciplined or rash, conscientious or irresponsible? The difference between an abundant life and an abysmal life is how you treat others (Romans 13:10).

The bottom line is thoughtful people enjoy the most satisfying lives. Most folks agree this simple philosophy makes sense. Christians concur but base their conviction on the surer evidence of Scripture. The Bible provides a principled shortcut to constructing a quality life. No extensive research is needed, and no lifetime of observation is required even though the Bible's teachings will resonate in your heart and be confirmed by your daily experience. One key to more love and more joy is more time in God's Word.

Truth is truth wherever you find it, but why take the long way around? Trial and error is the instructional method of choice for earth's slowest learners. There is no need to stumble and grumble through life when God has provided timeless wisdom in His Word (1 Thessalonians 2:13). Unbelief hinders spiritual and relational growth. Faith speeds your progress and maximizes your results (Romans 10:17). Therefore, to have the best possible life and the best possible relationships, "Trust in the Lord with all your heart" (Proverbs 3:5).

THE CONUNDRUM OF LOVE

Since the quality of your life depends on the quality of your relationships, what do you do when someone is a source of constant grief? Some people are dangerous to be around for any length of time (Matthew 7:6). They are narcissistic or parasitic. They use and abuse you but give little back. These are one-way, unsustainable, destructive relationships, so avoid them when possible and protect yourself if they are inescapable. It is not selfish to limit your exposure to those who spread misery rather than joy (Proverbs 22:24-25).

Avoiding unsafe people may sound unkind at first, but it is vital for preserving your integrity and sanity (Psalm 1). It is noble to seek the lost and serve the weak, but it is perilous to become intimate with someone unwilling to change his wicked ways. Paul cautioned that evil companions corrupt good morals (1 Corinthians 15:33) and warned against being unequally yoked together with unbelievers (2 Corinthians 6:14). When some- one claims to care for you but bases his decisions on his own interests, you are unequally yoked. In healthy relationships, friends look out for each other.

Be cordial to all, but do not be overly close with those who do not share your beliefs. To be emotionally or contractually obligated in a long-term relationship with someone who mocks your faith and undermines your values is a terrible mistake with painful consequences. Fleeing dangerous people and situations can be the wisest course of action (2 Timothy 2:22).

These quotes by George Washington express the seriousness of selecting an inner circle of friends:

"It is better to be alone than in bad company."

"Be courteous to all, but intimate with few, and let those few be well tried before you give them your confidence."

"True friendship is a plant of slow growth, and must undergo and withstand the shocks of adversity, before it is entitled to the appellation."

God allows you to choose your spouse and best friend. Choosing well is fundamental to well-being. You have numerous acquaintances but a small group of intimate allies with whom you spend most of your time. Ask yourself, "Does being around this person make me stronger or weaker?" By selecting a circle of friends who bring out the best in you, you build a social network that will sustain your soul. If that is what you want for your children, then is it not what God wants for His children?

THE CALLING OF LOVE

Even more important than choosing honorable associates is purposing to be considerate in your dealings with others.

Regardless of how you are treated, make up your mind to be courteous and kind to all (1 Peter 3:8). Never repay evil for evil. Instead, overcome evil with good (Romans 12:17-21). Jesus recommended three courses of action when people hurt you: pray for them, bless them, and do good to them (Luke 6:27-28). No matter what happens, do not stop loving them.

Christianity is a call to a considerate lifestyle modeled after Jesus' concern for others. His tenderheartedness led Him from heaven to the cross. Christ said, "If anyone desires to come after Me, let him deny himself, and take up his cross, and follow Me" (Matthew 16:24). In other words, quit thinking only of yourself. Following Christ requires putting the welfare of others before your own comfort and convenience. Consideration produces civility in society, productivity in the workplace, happiness in the home, and unity in the church. Considering one another is the welcome burden of a Christlike heart.

Considerateness

SELF-ASSESSMENT

Y N 1. Do I consider options and likely outcomes before speaking or acting?

Y N 2. Do I consider, "What is God's will in this decision?"

Y N 3. Do I consider, "What is your need at this moment?"

Y N 4. Do I consider, "What is my responsibility as a Christian?"

Y N 5. Do I consider, "What would I want if I were the other person?"

QUESTIONS

1. What is Jesus' number one rule for healthy relationships (Matthew 7:12)?

2. What is the basic skill of Christian living (Philippians 2:3-4)?

3. Name three Christ-approved courses of action when people hurt you (Luke 6:27-28).

4. What does consideration produce in society? At work? At home? In the church?

5. Kindness and forgiveness spring from what kind of heart (Ephesians 4:32)?

DISCUSSION

1. What signs do you see of growing incivility in society?

2. How will things improve when people become more considerate?

3. How do parents, teachers, and preachers teach empathy?

4. Why is success in life measured relationally?

5. What is the difference between civility and Christian consideration?

6. Can caring people protect themselves from unsafe people?

7. What happens when people obsess about their own images and interests?

8. What is the difference between an abundant life and an abysmal life?

EXERCISE

List three ways your congregation (or family) will become more considerate.

1

2

3

CHAPTER 2
Be Kind

When I was young, I admired clever people.
Now that I am old, I admire kind people.

—Abraham Joshua Heschel

Kindness can be hard work, requiring lots of thought and effort. You must deny yourself to attend the needs of others. So why would anyone bother? The more we understand the benefits of civility, the more inclined we are to pursue it. The more we minimize its value, the less motivated we are to cultivate a courteous lifestyle. Let us pause to remember why this endeavor is worth our time and effort.

BECAUSE IT IS NEEDED

God created human beings to need one another. Though we try to conceal our dependency, unmet needs lurk inside each of us. Some are physical, others are social, and many are spiritual. The good news is God gifted someone to help with our needs: a parent, teacher, coach, friend, minister, philanthropist, employer, colleague, businessman, professional, or brother in Christ. In addition to making us needy, He created someone who could assist in filling that need. You need to serve, and I need help.

Paul said, "We are His workmanship, created in Christ Jesus for good works, which God prepared beforehand that we should walk in them" (Ephesians 2:10). That means God created you with a unique capacity to serve others and a heart that finds fulfillment in doing good. It should come as no surprise that the ministry of Jesus consisted of going about doing good (Acts 10:38). Disciples of Christ have committed themselves to following in Jesus' footsteps by looking for ways to meet the needs of those God brings their way. Life consists of a series of human encounters that are opportunities to glorify God by doing good in His name.

Individuals need kindness, but so do societies. Civilization is not possible without citizens who rise above their selfish concerns. Compassion is as important to a nation's strength as its economy. Times of national emergency bring human sympathy to the surface. Recessions, earthquakes, storms, and famines bring out the best in many citizens.

The church is a spiritual society that requires consideration for its health and survival. The number one cause of division in the church is lack of love. Empathy is the basis of mercy, and apathy is the basis of misery. Without thoughtfulness and kindness, we inflict harm rather than bear burdens. Courtesy and charity are more than nice. They bond us together and build us up. There are many reasons to live considerately, but one of the greatest is this: it is sorely needed.

BECAUSE GOD COMMANDED IT

One of life's greatest pleasures is pleasing God. It is inexpensive and not overly complicated. It requires no special equipment or extensive training to get started. Just a little consideration and you are on your way to a great day. The fact that God commands consideration means it is good for you and the world.

There will always be reasons to withhold kindness. You are busy and more than a little tired. The recipient may be undeserving, and a background check may be in order. You already gave at the office or your place of worship.

So why do those warm impulses hang on with such tenacity? And why are they so painful to ignore? When you shrug them off, they trouble you at the oddest times of the day—and night. You wonder, "Why didn't I show more compassion?" There it was, an opening from God. A genuine human need. At that moment, my life mattered to someone. Make up your mind: "Next time, I will be ready to seize the moment."

BECAUSE GRATITUDE DEMANDS IT

John, the apostle of love, explained the basis of Christian charity in this way: "We love Him because He first loved us" (1 John 4:19). The motive behind every act of love is gratitude for blessings received. Gratitude is more inspiration than obligation. When you know how good it feels to be loved, you want others to share the joy. When you know how awful it feels to be hopeless, you will go to any length to spare someone that pain.

The love of God is seen in creation. The intricacies of the world's design show His interest in your happiness and well-being. The earth was filled with beauty for your enjoyment and not just your subsistence. There are over a hundred types of roses and a quarter of a million kinds of flowering plants. There are more than ten thousand species of birds ranging from the sprightly hummingbird to the ostentatious peacock to the colorful toucan to the awkward ostrich. Imagine the fun God had designing each one and thinking of the look on your face the first time you saw one. The flavors, fragrances, sounds, textures, and shapes of the created order exhibit an extravagance that could be founded only in divine love.

However, John was referencing the love of God in redemption rather than creation. Our understanding of love comes from the example of Christ at Calvary. It teaches us that we do not withhold love based on the actions of others. Instead, we love because we are children of God. Love is for the desperate and not just the deserving. Like John, Paul was intrigued by the gracious quality of divine love. He remarked, "For while we were still weak, at the right time Christ died for the ungodly" (Romans 5:6 ESV). What a perfect description of you and me: weak and ungodly. Though undeserving and helpless, God reached out to us in our wicked condition. It is the wonder of the ages and the mother of all motives.

BECAUSE YOU WILL LIKE YOURSELF MORE

It is hard to put a price tag on self-respect. What would you pay to feel great about yourself every day? What would it be worth to rid yourself of that nagging conscience that disapproves? How much would a great night's sleep be worth to you? How would you like to look at your face in the mirror and smile from ear to ear?

The more you are in control of your emotions and speech, the more you like yourself. The less you control your impulses, the lower your self-respect. Consideration helps you exercise more control over your life. It liberates you from selfishness so you can become who you want to be (Galatians 5:1). It allows you to anticipate the consequences of your actions, become a caring person, and create a kinder world.

Immature people are inconsiderate. Spiritually mature people are thoughtful and kind. Sympathy expands your mind and extends your influence. Self-control protects your relationships and refines your soul. It makes you appealing to others and at peace with yourself.

BECAUSE IT WILL IMPROVE YOUR HEALTH

I am not a physician, but I do read, and many books I come across proclaim the health benefits of good relationships. One thing I have never seen in print is someone arguing that kindness is detrimental to your health or that cruelty is highly beneficial. Evidence to the contrary is everywhere. Most doctors agree there is a correlation between good relationships and good health. Your body will thank you for becoming a calmer, more considerate person.

Not only can I read, but I can remember. I remember the times I was under stress because of conflict with someone, and I could not sleep. After a couple of days, I would come down with some ailment, usually the same one. It started in my throat, gravitated to my lungs, and then I would cough—for weeks. No one is immune to confirmation bias, so maybe the timing was just a coincidence, but experience tells me this: I feel better when I love better.

Solomon said, "A joyful heart is good medicine" (Proverbs 17:22a ESV). Anyone can be struck by illness, but the general rule is, the happier you are, the healthier you are. That is why the key to well-being is learning to relate well with others. Most episodes of unhappiness in your life can be traced to a difficult relationship with someone. Other than physical ailments, the greatest source of pain is a failed relationship.

BECAUSE IT WILL HELP YOU GET AHEAD

In business, the ability to get along with others is fundamental to meeting your career goals. In the long run, the manners you learned from your mom will serve you better than any degree or certification. Wise employers value workers with strong people skills. They recognize that etiquette and courtesy are not just nice, they are essential to building healthy teams that produce results.

Some fear that being nice will hamper their advancement in the workplace, but the genuinely considerate person has a broader, more enduring base of support than those who rely on intimidation. Humble people do not have to be doormats. Being courteous does not mean you cannot be appropriately assertive. Thinking before acting and choosing a fitting response demonstrates strength of character. Those who are in control of their mouths and emotions are more likely to be hired and promoted than those who are inconsiderate. Being a nice person cannot substitute for technical competencies, a good work ethic, or an innovative spirit, but all things being equal, it can be the difference maker in your career.

BECAUSE IT WILL BE RETURNED IN KIND

According to Paul, whatsoever a man sows, that shall he also reap (Galatians 6:7-10). The spiritual principle of reciprocity works relationally as well as morally. That means God wired people to respond to you in keeping with how you treat them. If you yell, they yell back. If you punch them in the nose, they come out swinging. But if you smile, most people instinctively return the favor. When you show a kindness, it will typically be repaid. When you send someone a card, they may respond in kind. When you open a door for others, they often hold the next one for you. Sure, these are little things, but the conclusion is clear. Life is more pleasant when you are pleasant.

CONCLUSION

What is clear is there are benefits for showing kindness and costs for ignoring human needs. Every day, you grow more considerate or callous. Insensitivity is not a normal condition. It is not human to see another's pain without your heart hurting, but the heart can grow hard if its promptings are repeatedly denied. By thinking more of yourself and less of others, you quiet your conscience and limit your capacity for empathy. Preoccupation with self is the death of the spirit. When love dies, the soul dies with it. When love grows, the soul revives. Consideration quickens the spirit. Moral feelings are heightened, and the imagination is awakened to its noblest purpose.

Sanctification begins with consideration, and consideration begins with awareness. The more I empathize with others, the more respectful and responsive I am to their needs. Christianity promotes an active interest in the welfare of others. It demands higher levels of thoughtfulness and responsibility than are common in society. Being considerate requires that grace and goodness triumph over apathy and ill will. It is long-term relational thinking over short-term selfish thinking.

But what does consideration look like on a practical level? How does the attitude translate into action? In the following chapters, you will find more examples of what it means to consider one another. Along the way, you will discover that "kindness is the greatest wisdom" (anonymous).

Kindness

SELF-ASSESSMENT

Y N 1. Do I believe in the practical benefits of behaving kindly?

Y N 2. Do I remember that kindness fulfills the purpose for which God made me?

Y N 3. Do I practice acting swiftly on impulses to show kindness (so I don't forget)?

Y N 4. Do I use kindness to say "thank You" to God for His kindness?

Y N 5. Do I recall how good it feels after I show someone kindness?

QUESTIONS

1. Why did John say we should love (1 John 4:19)?

2. What did Solomon say is good medicine (Proverbs 17:22)?

3. What does consideration free you from (Galatians 5:1)?

4. For whom did Christ die (Romans 5:6)?

5. According to Paul, what can a person expect to reap in life (Galatians 6:7-10)?

DISCUSSION

1. Why is kindness such hard work?

2. What are some signs God created us to need one another?

3. Why is lack of love a leading cause of division in the church?

4. What would you give to feel good about yourself every day?

5. How can you experience the same joy at a fraction of the cost?

6. Why do people fear that being nice at work will hamper their advancement?

7. How is consideration good medicine for the human condition?

8. Why is kindness the greatest wisdom?

EXERCISE

List three ways your congregation (or family) will become kinder.

1

2

3

CHAPTER 3
Be Friendly

Don't wait for people to be friendly, show them how.

—Author Unknown

When I go for a walk, I wave at every car and greet every pedestrian. I cannot help myself. It causes me pain to treat people as if they are invisible. I feel the same way in other settings. When someone enters a room, it is hard for me to ignore him. Instinctively, I look his direction, approach with hand extended, introduce myself, practice using his name, and ask questions to help us connect. When guests come for dinner, I watch their glasses to provide refills and their plates to offer seconds. If someone approaches a door where I am standing, I feel compelled to open it. If they are carrying something, I offer assistance.

My upbringing and faith have conditioned me to notice people and tend their needs. I still have blind spots and weak moments, but I thank God (and my wife) that I have come a long way in my battle against selfishness and laziness. The funny thing is I am the prime beneficiary of this outward focus. My marriage and career are more fruitful because of practicing consideration. Now, if I could just improve with those thank-you notes.

PAY ATTENTION

In the Garden of Gethsemane, Jesus told His disciples to watch and pray (Matthew 26:41), but when He returned, He found them sleeping. Peter, James, and John missed a priceless chance to comfort Christ in His hour of trial. I wonder, though, if we are dozing when it comes to occasions to serve Him by encouraging others (25:40). How many times do we overlook opportunities to assist people in their hour of need? Think of that newcomer to the congregation who is looking for a friendly face or that longtime member whose stooped shoulders cry out for support.

In *The Road Less Traveled*, M. Scott Peck explains, "The principal form that the work of love takes is attention." Life's best moments are the times we momentarily lose ourselves in caring for another, but before you can be considerate, you must first become conscious. Changing your behavior requires changing the focus of your attention. Kindness is preceded by caring, but you cannot care for someone you do not bother to notice. Nor can you engage in good works without imagining the suffering of the one you hope to alleviate. Your first responsibility as a Christian is to turn your heart toward God by sensing the needs of those around you (Matthew 25:40). Loving humanity is heaven's cure for vanity.

The essence of love is broadening your attention to care for those God brings into your presence. When you are watching your favorite football team, hear a child's cry, and rush to cradle him in your arms, that is love. When your mate wants spaghetti and you prefer fajitas, but you opt for Italian anyway, that is love. Self-denial in small things helps you grow the spiritual muscle necessary for Christlike love. It takes practice to have healthy relationships. To make room for someone in your life, you must first make room for him in your heart.

The essence of marriage, parenting, or friendship is giving others your attention. The basis of ministry and shepherding is less concern with self and more concern for others. At home, work, or play, you cannot be your best without social awareness. People who are oblivious have no concern for others. They are unaware of the way their words and deeds hurt others. They are insensitive to the struggles of those around them. Moreover, they have no inducement to change because they miss the subtle cues that more mindful people recognize.

Kindness is contingent on the awakening of your conscience. When you see others' needs and sense your responsibility, wonderful things happen. When you ignore people's pain and deny your accountability, wicked things occur. History's worst injuries and atrocities resulted from a combination of indifference and inattention. Apathy and insensitivity are responsible for most of the world's woes.

Heartlessness is dangerous to you and demeaning to others. Jesus illustrated this spiritual malady in the parable of the sower. When the heart is unfruitful, the problem is inattention. Hardheartedness is to God's Word what hard ground is to seed: a barrier to growth. Hardness occurs when there is too much concern for self and not enough concern for others. It was the sin of the rich man who overlooked the beggar at his gate (Luke 16:19-31). It is closing your eyes to someone's trouble when you could help if only you cared. John said,

> But if anyone has the world's goods and sees his brother in need, yet closes his heart against him, how does God's love abide in him? Little children, let us not love in word or talk but in deed and in truth. (1 John 3:17-18 ESV)

GREET ONE ANOTHER

When you encounter people, give them the gift of your attention from the start. Paul urged the Romans not to neglect the duty of greeting one another (Romans 16:16). In the long list of mankind's sins, failing to acknowledge another's presence seems like a minor slight bordering on insignificance. Yet under the inspiration of the Holy Spirit, in the precious space of an epistle preserved in the canon of Holy Scripture, an apostle of Jesus Christ reminded his readers of the importance of affirming one another through words and actions that express acceptance. Without these seemingly small gestures, there can be no community or harmony among believers.

Even a preschooler can master this powerful skill. I was on a late-night flight home when a little girl greeted every passenger as she sauntered down the aisle. Her mother eventually got up to retrieve her, and as she carried her daughter back to her seat, the grinning girl waved goodbye to everyone she met. You never saw so many smiles. In the twinkling of an eye, a plane full of grumpy adults was transformed into a jet full of jumbo smiles.

Do not underestimate the power of a gracious greeting. A warm welcome that sets others at ease is more than kind: it is obedience to God's will. A welcoming kiss is holy because it is doing spiritual work. The same can be said of a hug, handshake, or simple "hello." Sacred business is underway when your soul connects with another soul.

The main reason visitors do not return to a church is the lack of a warm reception. They may be ignored altogether, or the welcome may have seemed artificial and insincere. On a gut level, they did not feel loved. Biblical worship and sound teaching are necessary for church growth, but so is a friendly culture. A cold, unfeeling church conveys little of the Savior's love. Jesus said, "You will know them by their fruits" (Matthew 7:16), and the fruit of love, in its most basic form, is a simple, sincere greeting.

How many people choose to change their place of work for lack of a human connection? How many husbands work late and dread opening the door of their own houses for want of a warm embrace and word of appreciation? How many teenagers find their identity in a gang or some other group for lack of parental love and attention? Detachment is a defense mechanism for protecting wounded self-esteems. Aloofness says, "If you do not care about me, why should I care about you?" People desperately want to know that they matter. That is why few things are as painful and discouraging as being unnoticed.

People in the service industry know this feeling well. The lady behind the lunch counter, the cabbie behind the wheel, and the clerk behind the register are not viewed by social climbers as neighbors with families and feelings. The Golden Rule says to treat others how you would like to be treated if you were in their circumstances. So ask yourself, "How would it feel to be treated like you are not worth noticing? What would it do to your self-esteem? And if you routinely treat others this way, what do you think it does to your soul?"

Jesus is famous for loving the marginalized people of the first-century world: women and children, the diseased and disabled, tax collectors and sinners. All were received by Christ in a way that made them feel not only welcome but also special. When we are too busy or lazy or petty to affirm others, we are not following in Jesus' footsteps. To be Christ's disciple is to notice and care for people.

TIMING MATTERS

When my friend Jimmy England worked as a district pharmacy supervisor for Walgreens, he trained pharmacists to greet customers within fifteen seconds of their arrival. Some pharmacists avoid eye contact because they are insecure or because they are busy filling back orders. Regardless of the reason, it is seldom the right thing to do. Acknowledging the customer's presence buys time and goodwill. It sets him at ease and makes him feel important even though he must wait. A wave, wink, smile, or nod says, "You matter to me. I cannot serve you now, but I respect you and want to help you as soon as possible."

Jimmy believes the same thing is true about churches. The first time his wife, Anne, visited our congregation in Peachtree City, Georgia, he noticed her crying in Bible class. When he asked what was the matter, she said, "I know it's going to be all right." The welcome she received in the first minutes after her arrival won her heart. It felt like family. What makes a church family your family? Is it the preacher's style or the congregation's status? Peeling paint or thinly padded pews matter little when you feel loved and accepted.

Remember the anxiousness you felt when beginning a new job or moving to a new town. Fear and apprehension are natural responses to change. Though it is hard to leave familiar friends, handshakes and hugs on the other end can lessen the pain. When people smile at you and call your name, it reinforces your feelings of worth. When people avoid eye contact and keep their distance, you wonder, "What's wrong with me?" You feel dejected or angry. Few things are as agonizing as being overlooked.

THINK SMALL

Shortly after we were married, Lisa and I made a rule that we would give each other a kiss before leaving the house and immediately upon arriving home. No matter how big a hurry, no matter if the person is on the far end of the house, no matter how tired or mad we may be, we hunt each other down and greet one another with a kiss. This custom seems trivial to many people, but we find it solves lots of problems and keeps us a little closer when it would be easy to drift apart with our hectic schedules. Satisfaction in marriage has more to do with small acts of attention than big displays of pretension.

No extravagant event or expensive present can substitute for small daily doses of your attention. For instance, what could your children buy you that would do more for your heart than those enthusiastic greetings when you pull into the drive? Grinning from ear to ear, they run up to you and leap into your arms, excited to share the best news of the day. And if those greetings are precious to you, do you suppose God feels the same way? We are His children, and when we worship, we are greeting Him and kissing His face with praise before rushing into the workweek. I wonder how He feels when we start our day or week without a "hi" or "bye" or "I love You"?

Imagine the dread of the prodigal son on his long journey home (Luke 15:11-32). Was he more concerned about the pain of his humiliation or the pain he inflicted on his father? I think it was the latter. Looking into his father's eyes would be difficult, but they were the eyes he most needed to see. To his surprise, he saw grace there rather than judgment. Love brightens the eyes and comforts the hearts of those we greet.

After Adam and Eve ate the forbidden fruit, they went and hid. I know the feeling. After I was baptized as a freshman in college, it was only a short time till I gave in to my old sins. When I saw the professor who baptized me coming down the sidewalk, I would avert my eyes and walk hurriedly in the other direction. No matter how hard I tried to get away, he would run even harder to catch up and have a conversation. At first, I would feel awful, but before long, I was encouraged. He sensed my remorse and knew that piling on would not help. Instead, he would smile, greet me, and offer words of hope. His kindness and understanding gave me the will to press on. If he had not sought me out and greeted me graciously, I shudder to think where I would be today.

Paul said, "Bear one another's burdens, and so fulfill the law of Christ" (Galatians 6:2). Expressions of disapproval are necessary when a person will not admit wrongdoing, but censure is unnecessary and detrimental when a person is crushed beneath feelings of guilt. If we cannot love and affirm those who have stumbled and sinned, then Christianity is a fraud. Penitence is crucial, and sin cannot be ignored, but what people usually need is encouragement. Rebuking the guilt-ridden is like giving a drowning man a drink of water.

How can we save souls if we do not care enough to comfort hearts? If I do not care about your humanity, why should I concern myself with your eternity? People listen when they feel loved. When you see me, understand me, and feel me in your heart, then you have earned the right to be heard, but not until then.

The day is fast approaching when we will be greeted by Jesus and His angels as He returns to claim His followers and usher us into eternity. Then you will be greeted by God as you stand before His glorious throne. He will not ignore you or brush you off as He rushes to handle more interesting or pressing concerns. That moment of joy will surpass every earthly delight and cause all past sufferings to fade from memory. But never forget that every good thing you have become, every noble thing you have done, and every wonderful thing you will enjoy throughout eternity all began when someone who loved Jesus first spoke one simple word to you: "Hello!"

Friendliness

SELF-ASSESSMENT

Y **N** 1. Do I notice other people and set them at ease?

Y **N** 2. Do I approach people or wait for them to come to me?

Y **N** 3. Do I smile when I approach people?

Y **N** 4. Do I introduce myself and practice using the other person's name?

Y **N** 5. Do I ask questions to connect through understanding?

QUESTIONS

1. What is your first responsibility as a Christian (Matthew 25:40)?

2. What proves whether God's love is in your heart (1 John 3:17-18)?

3. What crowning command concludes Paul's letter to the Romans (16:16)?

4. What is the fruit of love in its most basic form (Matthew 7:16)?

5. How did Paul say we fulfill the law of Christ (Galatians 6:2)?

DISCUSSION

1. Why did God command us to greet one another?

2. Why is paying attention the principal form of the work of love?

3. Why is greeting one another sacred business?

4. What does failing to greet others do to them? To you?

5. What does failing to greet one another do to a church?

6. How do small gestures of love create community in churches?

7. How do small expressions of love create closeness in families?

8. What is the importance of timing in greetings?

EXERCISE

List three ways your congregation (or
family) will become friendlier.

1

2

3

CHAPTER 4
Be Compassionate

You cannot live a perfect day without doing something
for someone who will never be able to repay you.

—John Wooden

On a cold February day in 1952, a distress call came to the
Coast Guard Station in Chatham, Massachusetts, on Cape Cod.
During one of the worst storms ever to hit the East Coast, the
SS Pendleton oil tanker was ripped in half yet somehow remained
afloat. It was only a matter of time until she was going down.
More than thirty sailors were trapped on board with no way to
save themselves.

BERNIE'S CALL

Most of the life station crew were gone when the call came.
They were on a rescue mission to another foundering tanker, the
SS Fort Mercer. Bernie Webber, one of the few remaining crew-
men, was ordered by the station commander to pick a crew and
take the remaining lifeboat to rescue the stranded sailors on the
swiftly sinking *Pendleton.*

The sandbar between the Chatham Harbor and the open sea
is hazardous to navigate under the best of conditions. Now, the
storm was kicking up giant waves. Many considered the rescue
operation foolhardy, but Bernie would not be deterred. Men were
counting on him to cross over and come to their aid. He knew he
was their only hope of survival.

Timing the bursts of his engine to meet the battering waves, Bernie crossed the bar successfully but lost his compass in the jostling. Refusing to turn back, he steered in the general direction of the tanker and found his needle in a haystack. His small lifeboat was designed to carry twelve people, but unwilling to leave any man behind, Bernie managed to get thirty-two sailors on his craft. Shortly after the last man came aboard, the *Pendleton* went down. For his heroism, Bernie and his crew were awarded the Gold Lifesaving Medal.[1]

PAUL'S CALL

The apostle Paul was at Troas when a distress call arrived in the form of a night vision. He saw a man of Macedonia standing and urging him, "Come over to Macedonia and help us" (Acts 16:9b). When Paul saw the vision, he did not hesitate to answer the summons. Immediately, he and his lifesaving crew made arrangements to go to Macedonia. He knew God was calling him to preach the gospel to desperate men who could not save themselves. The gospel was their only hope.

YOUR CALL

These seafaring stories remind me of a familiar hymn by Charles Gabriel, "Send the Light." The song says, "There's a call comes ringing o're the restless wave: Send the light! Send the light! There are souls to rescue, there are souls to save: Send the light! Send the light!" Just as Bernie crossed over the bar and Paul crossed the Aegean Sea, we must be willing to cross over any barrier to reach the lost. Sometimes those obstacles are social and emotional rather than physical.

The final verse of Gabriel's song challenges worshippers: "Let us not grow weary in the work of love." The work of Christians is to show others the love of Jesus. This is done partly through

words but also through deeds. But there is a problem. Before
I can love you, I must risk knowing you. Love is about filling
human needs, and if I am to know what you need, I must get
close enough to find out what those needs are. I must cross over.

COURAGE TO CROSS OVER

In the parable of the good Samaritan (Luke 10:25-37), Jesus
celebrated the courage of a considerate man who dared to love a
stranger in need. The key phrase in this story is "the other side."
As kids, we all understood the sanctity of "my side" of the car. As
adults, we get familiar with "my side" of the auditorium. When
conflict arises, we defend "my side" of the debate. The "other
side" is your side, and that is where I must go to understand your
feelings and discover your needs. Until someone crosses over,
there can be no connection.

Crossing over can be wearisome, and frankly, I am more
comfortable here on my side. Knowing human nature and our
reluctance to cross over, Jesus told a compelling story to help
us experience the blessings of charity and intimacy. The alterna-
tive is an insular life of laziness and selfishness. Oddly, a life of
self-centeredness can be disguised as a life of religious devotion.
Jesus knew that the most religious are often the least likely to
cross over.

THE OCCASION

The backdrop of this parable was a question. A lawyer stood
and asked Jesus, "Teacher, what shall I do to inherit eternal life?"
(Luke 10:25). The man was not searching for answers. Rather, he
was looking for an angle to discredit Jesus. Nonetheless, the Lord
saw this as a perfect opportunity to teach about the essence of
true religion.

Knowing the man had come to trap Him rather than to learn, Jesus redirected the question: "What is written in the law? What is your reading of it?" (Luke 10:26). The scribe answered by quoting two familiar passages of Scripture: Deuteronomy 6:5 and Leviticus 19:18. "'You shall love the LORD your God with all your heart, with all your soul, with all your strength, and with all your mind,' and 'your neighbor as yourself'" (Luke 10:27).

Jesus commended the response and challenged him to practice what he had spoken. He told the lawyer, "You have answered rightly; do this and you will live" (Luke 10:28). Some satisfy themselves with knowing God's will. Jesus exhorted His listeners to do God's will. Embarrassed by the way Jesus turned the tables on Him, the lawyer attempted to save face by asking a follow-up question: "And who is my neighbor?" Now the table was set for telling one of the greatest stories of all time.

THE SET

The setting for the story was the road from Jerusalem to Jericho. Jerusalem is 2,300 feet above sea level while Jericho is 1,300 feet below sea level. Consequently, the road drops 3,600 feet in less than twenty miles. It is narrow, rocky, twisting, and dangerous. Jesus' listeners knew this hazardous road was a favorite of criminals, who would lie in wait for unsuspecting travelers. Instantly, the tension began to build.

THE CAST

The story consisted of four main characters, beginning with a hapless traveler who was ambushed and abandoned. Thieves beat him, robbed him, and stripped him before leaving him half-dead. A priest happened by the crime scene, but chose to pass by without offering assistance. Shortly thereafter, a Levite came upon the victim, but also hurried past. Jesus' listeners must have been disturbed by the indifference of these respected religious men. If anyone should help the helpless, it ought to be them. The priest and Levite passed by more than a man that day. They also passed by an opportunity to grow spiritually, do good, and glorify God.

Next, Jesus introduced the unlikely hero of the story, a kind-hearted Samaritan. Samaritans were despised by Jews because of their mixed blood and misguided worship, and that is precisely why Jesus made him His leading man. The contrast was sharp and clear: religion versus righteousness, holiness in form or in fact (2 Timothy 3:5). Jesus was not condoning everything about the Samaritan, but He was commending his compassion. No doubt, his religion was confused, but his heart was tender and his motives sincere.

THE CLIMAX

The story reached its climax when the Samaritan stumbled upon the wounded man. The priest and Levite chose to pass by on "the other side." What would a man of inferior religious training choose to do? When he saw him, instead of passing by, he went to "his side." Compassion enabled him to cross over. He set aside his fears, prejudices, and agenda for the day to help a fellow human being in his time of need.

The Samaritan started by bandaging the injured man's wounds, treating them with oil and wine. Then he set him on his own animal, walked alongside, and led him to an inn. The Samaritan did not abandon his patient. Instead, he personally took care of him for the remainder of the day. Before setting out on the following morning, the Samaritan paid the innkeeper to continue the care and promised to make up any difference when he returned. So the heartwarming story came to an end.

THE QUESTION

However, Jesus was not finished. Turning to the lawyer whose question began the exchange, He asked, "So which of these three do you think was neighbor to him who fell among the thieves?" (Luke 10:36). The answer was undeniable: "He who showed mercy on him" (v. 37). The neighbor was the one who crossed over to the other side. The secret to understanding this parable lies in the words "the other side." You cannot pass by a person without closing your heart to him. Something was definitely wrong in the hearts of the thieves who injured the traveler but also in the hearts of those who ignored his desperate situation.

I am comfortable on "my side." Your side is uncomfortable because it brings me in contact with your needs, your feelings, and your very soul. The priest and Levite feared getting too close to the injured man because, if they got to know him, their hearts would not let them pass. To pass him by, they had to keep their distance physically and emotionally. Why? Because intimacy not only connects people, it also obligates them (Romans 13:8). It is hard to dismiss you once I know you, so I will ignore you.

The priest and Levite passed by because they were not asking the right question. They were thinking, "What will happen to me if I help?" That is to say, what risk, expense, and inconvenience might I incur? A better question is, "What will happen to him if I do not help?" One question focuses on personal gains and losses; the other, on human need. The Samaritan's heart instantly led him into action to relieve suffering. He did not debate or drag his feet. He could not help himself. Questions were replaced by action.

THE CHALLENGE

The concluding words of Christ are the most challenging. Jesus said to the lawyer (and to us), "Go and do likewise" (Luke 10:37). Now you have the lesson. It is time to start crossing over.

God's people are always crossing over. Abraham left Ur and crossed over to Canaan. Moses left Egypt and crossed over the Red Sea. Joshua left Moab and crossed over the Jordan River. In each case, they crossed over to create a better future for the people of God. They left the familiar for the unfamiliar in hopes of something better.

Hearts that are hardened lack the empathy needed to cross over and bless others. Pharaoh could not cross over racial divides to identify with the Hebrew slaves he oppressed. The rich man could not cross over social divides to feel the pain of poor Lazarus, who sat starving at his gate. When the heart crosses over, helping hands follow.

Christians must not injure others like the thieves, but neither can they ignore others like the priest and Levite. Moved with compassion, Christlike people intervene on behalf of those who are hurting. Sometimes that suffering is physical, and saints provide food, shelter, clothing, or medicine. Sometimes the suffering is emotional, and disciples provide comfort, encouragement, and good company. At other times, the suffering is spiritual, and believers provide hope and peace through the gospel of Jesus.

As people travel the twisting road of life, there are many hazards along the way. Besides ordinary dangers, there are spiritual bandits who lie in wait. Jesus said the thief comes to steal, kill, and destroy (John 10:10a). The wicked strip people of their dignity, rob them of their purity, and dash their hope of eternity. When you encounter wounded souls, how far will you go to help them in their time of need?

THE CONCLUSION

The gospel is the story of Jesus crossing over to our side. His side was heaven. Our side was a world hopelessly lost in sin. Jesus' heart would not let Him pass by on the other side. Augustine looked beyond the ethical lessons in the parable of the good Samaritan to suggest that the hero of the story was Christ Himself. Regardless of whether you agree, the parallels are striking. Like the Samaritan, Jesus was despised, paid for our healing, gave us to the care of the church, and will soon return.

In the end, you will not be judged solely on the number of religious services you attended. Rather, it will be based on the life you lived in relation to your fellow man. To whom did you show compassion? Whom did you relieve or rescue? We know the choice of the priest and the Levite, who thought they were honoring God but did not understand His purpose and priorities. We know the choice of the Samaritan, who went above and beyond to render assistance regardless of the cost and inconvenience (Colossians 3:14).

So what will you do with the opportunities God affords you? Satan will try to distract and confuse you about your mission. Are religious gatherings your highest priority? Do not forsake assembly times, but do not mistake their purpose. God is pleased when you praise Him in song, but He is even more delighted when you love someone in His name after the assembly has ended. Jesus said, "Go and do likewise." Go now. Do not hesitate or vacillate. By all means, do not pass by. Instead, deny yourself. Go the second mile. Cross over!

Compassion

SELF-ASSESSMENT

Y   N   1. Do I accept that loving well is hard work?

Y   N   2. Do I risk loving people who may not love me
in return?

Y   N   3. Do I often leave my comfort zone and cross over into
the worlds of others?

Y   N   4. Do I truly love my neighbor as myself?

Y   N   5. Do I replace inner debate with action?

QUESTIONS

1. What two verses did the scribe cite in answer to Jesus' question
(Luke 10:27)?

2. Who passed by the injured man in Jesus' story
(Luke 10:31-32)?

3. Who stopped to help the man (Luke 10:33)?

4. Who did the scribe say was neighbor to the waylaid traveler (Luke 10:37)?

5. What was Jesus' instruction to the scribe (Luke 10:37)?

DISCUSSION

1. Before I can love you, why must I risk knowing you?

2. Why are people hesitant to cross over?

3. Why did the priest and Levite fail to cross over?

4. Why did Jesus make a Samaritan the hero of His story?

5. What did the Samaritan set aside to render assistance?

6. What impresses you most about the Samaritan?

7. How is the gospel the story of Jesus crossing over?

8. Why could Jesus not pass by on the other side?

EXERCISE

List three ways your congregation (or family)
will become more compassionate.

1

2

3

CHAPTER 5
Be Present

Those who bring sunshine to the lives
of others cannot keep it from themselves.

—James Matthew Barrie

If loving is the greatest commandment, then listening is the greatest responsibility. Every act of kindness begins with noticing someone's need, and listening well is critical to knowing others' needs. That is why your ears are your best tools for displaying God's love. Ears are not the most attractive part of the human body, but when used well, they make you highly attractive to other people.

The reason we do not love well is because we do not listen well. Ears are God's most underutilized gift to mankind. The reasons for poor listening are usually cultural and spiritual rather than physical. Caring actions occur when your ears are finely tuned to the frequency of love.

THE CULTURAL CHALLENGE

The cultural challenge to listening well is distraction. Anything that keeps you from giving your full attention to what is most important at a given moment is a distraction. Distraction prevents you from hearing what you need to hear. It diverts your attention so that lesser things take priority over greater things.

We live in the age of distraction. Never has there been more mental clutter than in recent times. Drivers are watching movies rather than watching the road. Joggers are listening to music instead of approaching motorcars. Workers text and browse throughout meetings so that a fraction of their attention is directed to solving the problem at hand. Not only do they miss important details, but they also miss connecting with those who are present.

Never before have so many people been looking down, not in humility or prayer but in digital diversions. Something is lost when you see the tops of people's heads more than their eyes. Trying to communicate with someone whose eyes are averted and whose attention is divided is frustrating and discouraging. You feel disrespected.

THE SPIRITUAL CHALLENGE

The spiritual challenge to listening well is selfishness. Selfishness occurs when you are more concerned with your own interests than the well-being of others. When you listen better, you grow spiritually as well as relationally. Practicing this skill requires you to shift your focus from self to others. It requires clear intention and constant effort, and that is why good listening is a sign of inward change. To succeed, you must train yourself to listen strategically and compassionately.

Listen Strategically

Solomon classified poor listeners as foolish (Proverbs 18:2) and exceptional listeners as wise (v. 15). The difference between a good listener and a poor one is not their intelligence but their attentiveness. A person with an average IQ who listens well has a better quality of life than a distracted, self-indulged genius. Wise people are strategic listeners. They listen

- thoroughly to avoid jumping to conclusions (v. 13).

- eagerly to avoid impulsive commitments (v. 2).
- impartially to avoid bias and favoritism (v. 17).

Listen Compassionately

Besides listening strategically, Christians must also listen compassionately. There is no greater encouragement to improve your listening skills than the example of the Godhead. The One who heard the cries of His people in bondage still hears the cries of His children in distress (1 Peter 5:7). The One who heard the pleas of the blind man by the roadside still hears the pleas of those who long to see spiritually (Ephesians 5:14). The One who heard the hearts of believers on Pentecost still hears the hearts of those overwhelmed by life's problems (Romans 8:26). A sure way to become more God-like, Christ-like, and Spirit-like is to listen like the Father, Son, and Holy Spirit. When you love someone, you hang on their words. You hear what they say but also what they do not say. Love enables you to hear the unspoken words of the heart.

Nothing will change your life better or faster than improving your listening skills. It is the key to more civility in society and more success in your personal life. Listening well can improve your marriage and career. Your boss will like it, and your spouse will love it. It will make you a better parent and friend. It will increase your effectiveness in serving and in sharing your faith. In other words, it makes you better at nearly everything you do.

The costs of poor listening are a decline of clear thought and meaningful relationships. Conversely, the benefits of exceptional listening are more clarity and closeness. The choice is yours. You can be a "talkaholic" or a "hearaholic." Wonderful things happen to your family and friendships when you become a passionate listener. It takes hard work to make this change permanent, but the blessings are worth the effort.

Most people think they are better than average listeners (the same people consider themselves above average in good looks and driving ability). The fact that they think this may be the biggest obstacle they face in improving their listening skills. Admitting you have a problem is the first step to solving it. Face it: you are not the world's greatest listener, and you have more than a little room for improvement. So how badly do you want to change, and if you will not do it for yourself, will you do it for those you love?

Poor listening is a sin at some level because it is a sign of selfishness. It misses the mark of love and violates the boundaries of healthy relationships. There are three common ways you can harm others by failing to listen (Proverbs 10:19): dominating conversations, giving unsolicited advice, and listening superficially.

DOMINATING CONVERSATIONS

Spiritually healthy people talk to communicate, connect, and collaborate. Unhealthy people talk excessively to satisfy their egos. Inordinate talkers are motivated by selfishness and insecurity. They speak more than is normal or desirable. A person who rambles does so for the pleasure it gives him without considering the pain it causes others.

Speedy Talkers

Speedy talkers are easy to spot. They are unable to stay on track unless the subject interests them. They may be charming at first, but their tactics make them tiresome as time passes. They are prone to interrupt what you are saying to share their own thoughts, which they deem more important. In addition, they frequently and abruptly change topics to match their own concerns. *To avoid being rude, practice giving others the spotlight.*

Needy Talkers

Insecure talkers cannot stand silence. Consequently, they rehash what they already said over and over without adding much new. Their nervousness is plain to see. Their tension is driven by an obsession with your opinion of them. They are trying to impress you. When someone repeats himself a lot, he is probably self-conscious to a fault. *To avoid being annoying, practice saying less and enjoying silence.*

Greedy Talkers

Greedy talkers are overdependent on others emotionally. They are ravenous for your attention and admiration. Like a sinkhole, the psychological void is impossible to fill, so when they latch onto you, they will not let go. They drain you emotionally by clinging and prattling. If you give them an hour of your attention or a whole day, it is never enough. Unconsciously fearing abandonment, they press the "conversation" beyond its natural limits. Every time you politely try to break free, they use every tactic to reel you back into their verbal clutches. Sadly, their strategies backfire and repel people. Fearful you cannot escape, you begin ducking them altogether. *To avoid being disagreeable, practice letting go.*

Do you tend to dominate conversations? Do you keep talking long after people have mentally checked out? If you are not sure, look for these common signs. Tired listeners begin checking the time. Once may be a coincidence, but if you catch them gazing at the clock a second time, it is a sure sign you have gone over the limit. Another clue is doughnut eyes. Not big and round but glazed over like a Krispy Kreme doughnut. Backing up is another clue. If you wish your listener would be still because you have to follow him around to keep his attention, you are the one who is not listening. Fatigued listeners look away, back up, fidget, multitask, read, type, text, and straighten. Occasionally, they give verbal hints such as "I've gotta run" or "I was just headed out." Yawning and snoring may also be clues.

When you lose your manners, you may also lose respect and a friend. Talking too much can be rude, mildly irritating, or even obnoxious. It is your responsibility to keep things in balance. Practice being brief without being curt. Ask more questions and work on being more curious than chatty. The key to healthy relationships is give and take. The goal is dialogue, and the impediment is monologue. When you stop trying to impress people, things rapidly improve. When you become genuinely interested in others, the imbalance naturally corrects itself. The fascinating thing is that the less you dominate the conversation, the more you like people, and the more they like you.

The Bible compares communication to riding a horse (James 1:26). The rider uses a bridle to guide or stop the horse. Without a bridle, the horse may run away with the rider. When the tongue is not bridled, the mouth may run away with the speaker. The point is you can control your speech, and sometimes the best thing you can do is put on the brakes. When you dominate the conversation for more than a minute, your chances of boring or alienating the hearer increase with every second that passes. The greater your soul and the purer your religion, the better you listen.

GIVING UNSOLICITED ADVICE

When someone shares a problem with you, avoid the temptation to offer quick and easy solutions. Do not interrupt the speaker or hint that you have quit listening and would like for him to hurry up so you can share the obvious answer. Listen patiently and thoroughly.

In most cases, people are perfectly capable of handling the situation when they are ready. They did not come to you for advice. They came to you for sympathy and emotional support. Offering cheap advice that costs you nothing can make a person feel lonelier rather than motivated.

If you feel compelled to share your ideas, ask permission first. Make sure the hearer is ready to move into problem-solving mode. Better yet, wait until he asks. There are times to give a struggling person unsolicited advice, but most of the time, it is the last thing he needs. Give him your presence and encouragement but hold your tips until the time is right.

LISTENING SUPERFICIALLY

You are to love God with *all* your heart, mind, strength, and soul. If listening is loving, then you need to listen with your entire being as well. Listening wholeheartedly is hard work. Becoming a passionate listener takes lots of energy. To do it well, you must give it your all. That means you must stop attempting to do other things at the same time. Three energy zappers to avoid are judging, solving, and rehearsing. Resist the temptation to exit listening mode and move prematurely into problem-solving or practicing mode. And here is where the best listeners excel: when the other person finishes speaking, before you jump in, pause and encourage him to say more. Do this as many times as he will continue.

Too many people are stuck in superficial relationships where real understanding cannot occur. When colleagues and couples are in conflict, the problem may be that they have not worked hard enough to know each other. Where is the love in a relationship? It is in the details and dreams. The harder you work to know someone on a soul level, the more good things occur. The less I know you, the easier it is to misunderstand you. Surface listening makes a person feel unsafe and unimportant. Deep listening lets people know you truly care.

FOCUS

When I spend more time thinking about my needs than your needs, trouble is coming. Listening well will not solve every problem, but it is the right place to begin. To do this, you may need to simplify and slow down. Focus on one thing and one person at a time.

Three obstacles can keep you from connecting with others because they keep you from listening well. Talking too much, advising too much, and assuming too much are hurdles of the heart. Practice listening to get your ears in shape so you can leap past the hurdles that lie in the path to another's heart. By doing this, you avoid interrupting, convey interest, and move the conversation to a deeper level. Most people do not share their true feelings until you convince them you care. Good listening closes the emotional distance between two people. Listening is the ultimate "lover's leap."

Presence

SELF-ASSESSMENT

Y N 1. Do I accept that listening well is inseparable from loving well?

Y N 2. Do I listen thoroughly to avoid bias and jumping to conclusions?

Y N 3. Do I practice giving others the spotlight in our conversations?

Y N 4. Do I practice saying less rather than nervously repeating myself?

Y N 5. Do I practice letting people go rather than clinging or nagging?

QUESTIONS

1. When words are many, what is not lacking (Proverbs 10:19)?

2. In what does a fool take pleasure (Proverbs 18:2)?

3. What can the Holy Spirit hear (Romans 8:26)?

4. What should Christians do with their tongues (James 1:26)?

5. Who is the best model of good listening (1 Peter 5:7)?

DISCUSSION

1. What are signs that we live in an age of distraction?

2. Why is listening hard work?

3. Why is talking too much a spiritual problem?

4. Why is offering unsolicited advice a bad idea?

5. Why is speech a leading measure of your religion?

6. How do you give others the spotlight?

7. How can you learn to enjoy silence?

8. How is listening the ultimate lover's leap?

EXERCISE

List three ways your congregation (or family) will practice presence.

1

2

3

CHAPTER 6
Be Courteous

Life is short, but there is always time enough for courtesy.

—Ralph Waldo Emerson

Jesus was a social man. The Gospels record His presence at public and private functions. He attended at least one wedding and was a frequent guest at banquets. Sometimes, the dinners were hosted by those on the fringes of Israelite society (publicans), but He also received invitations to dine at the homes of more prominent people (Pharisees).

Jesus was aware of different motives behind these requests. Some wanted to get to know Him, and others wanted to destroy Him. In either case, Jesus knew He was being closely watched. He was also observing the behavior of His dinner companions. His aim was not to embarrass them with petty criticisms but to elevate them through dialogue about their conduct. How they reacted to His comments revealed the condition of their hearts.

THE SETTING

Luke 14:7-14 tells the story of one such encounter. While attending a dinner party, Jesus noted the way guests jockeyed for positions at the table. In the first century, seating arrangements were taken very seriously. The host would assign seats, and proximity to the host was an indication of special regard.

On this occasion, no seating chart had been arranged in advance. As a result, the guests were left to select their own seats at the table. Jesus watched as attendees gravitated toward higher rather than lower positions. They were unaware that this simple choice sent an unmistakable message about their philosophy of life.

THE TEACHING

At an opportune moment, Jesus addressed the group and shared His thoughts about this faux pas. Since it was common for prominent guests to arrive late, it was unwise to assess your social ranking and choose a seat based on who was present at the time of your arrival. Besides, even if no one arrived after you, your evaluation might differ from that of the host, and this could lead to an embarrassing situation. To be unseated and downgraded in the presence of your peers could be a mortifying experience.

The good news is this blow to your self-esteem is totally avoidable. All you have to do is humble yourself before someone else does it for you. Jesus' advice was to intentionally select the lowest possible place when the choice is left to your discretion. By doing this, there is little danger of being demoted and an excellent chance the host will ask you to move up.

THE SURFACE MEANING

Jesus' teaching sounds like one of the simple rules for wise living you might find in the book of Proverbs. In fact, a very similar teaching can be found in Proverbs 25:6-7:

> Do not exalt yourself in the presence of the king, and do not stand in the place of the great; for it is better that he say to you, "Come up here," than that you should be put lower in the presence of the prince, whom your eyes have seen.

On one hand, Jesus said if you look at this scenario purely from the point of self-interest, you ought to know better than to exalt yourself. Life experience tells you it will not produce the results you want. Any thoughtful person should know better. But Jesus had more in mind than avoiding a bruised ego or securing a box seat. Clearly, more is going on here than meets the eye.

THE DEEPER MEANING

Everyone commits social blunders from time to time, but when indiscretion is a lifestyle rather than a gaffe, there is reason for concern. Lack of etiquette and decorum reveal a more basic problem. More than lapses in judgment, they evidence selfishness. Jesus' chief concern with His fellow guests was not the specific transgression under discussion. Rather, it was the underlying "me first" attitude that springs from a proud heart.

Pride produces a preoccupation with self. When you value yourself above others and think of yourself before others, the result is insensitivity or cruelty. Even when "kindness" is extended, it is self-serving rather than sincere. Your concern is with how you appear rather than doing good to others (Ephesians 6:5-6).

Empathy is a God-given capacity to understand the feelings of others. Pride mutes this sensitivity until the pleadings of the conscience become white noise rather than an urgent alarm. Conceit short-circuits the spiritual wiring of the heart and turns your inner voice into a mild nuisance that is easily suppressed. With the conscience out of the way, it is possible to frame selfish acts as sensible and deserving.

The solution to selfishness and impoliteness is humility. True humility is not demeaning yourself but, rather, respecting others. By thinking realistically about yourself, you make room for others in your heart. When you think of me and care for me, you are more likely to treat me with dignity.

Jesus concluded His remarks with a Hebrew maxim from Proverbs 29:23: "Whoever exalts himself will be humbled, and he who humbles himself will be exalted" (Luke 14:11). In either case, you will be humbled. The only question is whether you will do it yourself or someone must impose it on you. Embrace humility or suffer humiliation: the choice is yours. Jesus was commending self-examination and preemptive action. Do not wait to be shamed. Being proactive is less painful and more profitable.

HUMILITY IN ACTION

The result of true humility is a "you first" attitude. So what does humility look like in daily life? At the workplace, it is waiting for others to exit the elevator rather than barging in as soon as the doors open. On the road, it is driving in the right lane unless you are passing another car no matter how much you paid in taxes. In the family, it is letting someone else decide what to watch or where to eat. At the coffee shop, it is leaving the seat by the outlet for someone else if you have a full charge on your laptop battery and, if not, choosing the bottom plug to leave easier access for the next guy. In marriage, it is letting your spouse have the new car while you drive the museum piece or fixing up the nursery when you wanted a motorcycle.

"You first" is opening and holding doors. It is putting the seat down on the bathroom commode. It is going last in line but never taking the last piece of pie. It is saying "May I?", "please," and "thank you." "You first" is waiting till everyone is seated before you begin to eat and waiting till everyone is finished before leaving the table. It is asking someone "What do you think?" and listening intently as she speaks. Putting others first is a habit that comes with spiritual growth and lots of practice.

Selfishness dies hard, but you can overcome it with deep desire and divine help (Romans 8:13).

Mac McAnally sings a heartwarming song called "You First" that tells the story of two brothers during three periods of their lives. While teenagers, they dared each other, "you first," when swimming the span of a local river. Later, as soldiers, both were wounded in battle. When the chopper arrived to evacuate casualties, they discovered there was room for only one more. This time, "you first" carried a different meaning that comes only with maturity. In the final snapshot, one brother is lying at the side of his sibling's deathbed, wishing he could swap places. He never dreamed it would be "you first."

Following each scene, the chorus repeats, "You first, and I'll be right behind you. You first, I'll meet you on the other side." Whether the other side is a riverbank, a hospital, or heaven, those who live life best are those who know the meaning of "You first." By putting Christ first in your heart, you will find it easier to put others there as well.

THE ULTIMATE MEANING

Minding your manners and putting others first will please God and help you get along in the world, but Jesus' message can be interpreted on a third and higher level. Along with practical advice for better living, Jesus used banqueting images to represent bigger themes. He was giving His hearers food for thought about God's eternal kingdom and their place in it. The more you think about it, the story moves from behavior to attitude to faith; or from me first to you first to Him first.

In Jesus' kingdom parables, the host of the banquet is often God Himself. In this parable about pushy guests, Jesus may have been hinting about those who were pushing Him aside in pursuit of personal prestige. The Pharisees and Sadducees wanted positions of power close to God and placed themselves above Christ to hold on to them at all costs. In doing so, they also placed themselves above those they were supposed to serve on God's behalf.

If anyone could teach this lesson on giving up the best seats, it was Jesus. Before coming to earth, He was seated with God in heaven. He humbled Himself and gave up His seat to come to earth and save mankind. In place of a throne surrounded by angels, He chose a manger surrounded by sinners. You cannot go lower. But after His death on the cross, He was raised from the grave, and the Host of Heaven said, "Come up higher" (cf. Philippians 2:9). In stark contrast, those who exalt themselves will lose their place at God's table when Christ returns to judge the world. Like prideful angels (Jude 6), self-promoters will be excluded from heaven's banquet and the joy of the redeemed (Matthew 8:11-12).

APPLYING THE LESSON

The New Testament is filled with inspiring examples of those who understood and lived by the principle Jesus taught. John the Baptist displayed a "Him first" attitude when he declared, "He must increase, but I must decrease" (John 3:30). Paul demonstrated a "Him first" philosophy when he announced, "But whatever gain I had, I counted as loss for the sake of Christ" (Philippians 3:7 ESV).

Moses exhibited a "Him first" outlook when he gave up the throne of Egypt for the greater glory of serving God's people (Hebrews 11:23-27). The entire eleventh chapter of Hebrews is the Bible's "Him first" memorial, celebrating the commitment of those who suffered harassment, deprivation, and torture for putting the Lord first in their lives. These humble servants will be called into God's presence to receive honor and blessings for time unending (Micah 6:8).

It is God's prerogative to determine who will receive seats of honor in His eternal kingdom (Mark 10:40). He is the host of the banquet, and seating arrangements will not be determined by your pushiness (Romans 9:16), pleading (Matthew 7:21-23), or high opinion of yourself (Luke 18:9-14). However, those who are truly humble will be pleasantly surprised to find places prepared for them around the table of the Lord (Matthew 25:37; John 14:1-3).

HEAVENLY PLACES

The parable of the best seats is many stories in one. First, it illustrates the silliness and impracticality of "me first" behavior. Next, it demonstrates the beauty and advantages of a "you first" attitude. Finally, it concludes with the glory and blessings of a "Him first" faith. The most amazing thing is that when you adopt a "Him first" faith, you do not have to wait to enjoy heaven's best seats. Paul explained,

> But God, who is rich in mercy, because of His great love with which He loved us, even when we were dead in trespasses, made us alive together with Christ (by grace you have been saved), and raised us up together, and made us sit together in the heavenly places in Christ Jesus. (Ephesians 2:4-6)

When you humble yourself and allow Jesus to take His place on the throne of your heart, you will be raised up from the waters of baptism to take your place among the redeemed. Those who are raised to newness of life are privileged to sit in the best seats one can enjoy this side of eternity: heavenly places in Christ Jesus.

Though your body remains on earth, your heart, mind, and soul can travel ahead and take their place in the glory of glories. When you worship God in spirit and truth, you are already there. When you set your affection on things above, you are already there. When you deny yourself, take up your cross, and follow Him, you are already there. The limitations of flesh and blood cannot keep your spirit from journeying to its true home, where it will await your resurrected body. Anytime you want them, the best seats are yours to enjoy. Just humble yourself, lift up others, and listen for the invitation to "come up higher."

Courtesy

SELF-ASSESSMENT

Y N 1. Do I often exhibit a "me first" attitude?

Y N 2. Do I frequently adopt a "you first" mindset?

Y N 3. Do I regularly display a "Him first" faith?

Y N 4. Do I spend much time sitting in heavenly places?

Y N 5. Do I believe that, if I humble myself, God will
         lift me up?

QUESTIONS

1. What should you not do at a banquet (Proverbs 25:6-7)?

2. What two things did Paul warn servants to avoid
   (Ephesians 6:5-6)?

3. What will happen to a person who exalts himself
   (Proverbs 29:23)?

4. What did God do after Jesus humbled Himself
   (Philippians 2:9)?

5. Where are Christians seated upon their conversion (Ephesians 2:4-6)?

DISCUSSION

1. What do manners tell you about a person?

2. Why did God create humans with a capacity for empathy?

3. How does pride affect the conscience?

4. Why is humility the solution to selfishness and impoliteness?

5. What does humility look like in daily life?

6. Explain the maxim "Embrace humility or suffer humiliation."

7. How did Jesus demonstrate giving up the best seats?

8. What does it feel like to sit in heavenly places today?

EXERCISE

List three ways your congregation (or family) will become more courteous.

1

2

3

CHAPTER 7
Be Merciful

*Beginning today, treat everyone you meet as if they were
going to be dead by midnight. Extend to them all the care,
kindness, and understanding you can muster, and do it with
no thought of any reward. Your life will never be the same again.*

—Og Mandino

The minor prophet Micah issued a memorable challenge to
the people of his generation. Many were religious, but few were
righteous. Forms of religion were abundant, but the heart was
missing. Cutting through the confusion, Micah provided a simple
description of true religion by highlighting three essentials for
pleasing God and living a holy life:

> He has shown you, O man, what is good; and what does the
> LORD require of you but to do justly, to love mercy, and to
> walk humbly with your God? (Micah 6:8)

What is good? What is required? These are strong words
intended to make readers sit up and take notice. Micah sifted
through all the details of the Jewish religion to determine what is
essential. What is the heart of the matter? What is this God thing
all about? He decided it basically comes down to three things:
justice, mercy, and humility. In other words, be fair, be gracious,
and be meek. Those who are equitable, merciful, and correctable
are on the right spiritual path.

These three essentials may seem unconnected, but they are closely linked. To walk humbly with God means you want to please Him more than anything else in the world. How is that possible except by treating your fellow man as He intended? When you take advantage of others, He is displeased. When you close your heart to their needs, He is saddened. When you drift from His purpose for your life, He nudges you back on track, but you must be open to His teaching and discipline. This is where humility comes into play. You must be correctable. A willingness to change and improve is a core component of true religion. To grow spiritually is to become a more compassionate and servant-hearted person, and this requires openness to God's promptings.

Being humble is the key to living a merciful life. To do this, Micah said you must "love" mercy. To make a significant change in any area of your life, you must be passionate about it. Lasting change requires a deep desire to improve. You seldom become a better person by accident. Achieving goals requires an eager longing to reach your aim. When your greatest delight is to become a more caring and helpful person, you are bound to succeed.

Mercy is critical because everyone needs it. Blessed are those who bring relief to the distressed and forgiveness to the guilty. Mercy goes beyond treating others justly (not burdening others). It is treating others compassionately (unburdening others). The question is, "How can I learn mercy?"

In Kansas City, a thirteen-year-old boy was walking home from school when he noticed he was being followed by two older teens. He hurried to reach the safety of his house, but as he got to the front porch and was struggling to open the front door, they overtook him. Dousing him with gasoline, the attackers said, "This is what you deserve. You get what you deserve." Then they flicked a lighter. The victim survived the attack, but the physical and emotional scars remain.[2]

Mercy is something you learn, which means it must be taught. Sadly, some children grow up in a home where they learn intolerance rather than kindness and goodness. In retrospect, you wish someone like Micah had been present in the attackers' younger lives to teach them to love mercy.

GOD'S MERCY

Imagine how things might have turned out differently that day had a parent taught the attackers about God's mercy as they were growing up. Before going to bed, they might have read aloud passages like these:

Blessed be the God and Father of our Lord Jesus Christ, the Father of mercies and God of all comfort, who comforts us in all our tribulation, that we may be able to comfort those who are in any trouble, with the comfort with which we ourselves are comforted by God. (2 Corinthians 1:3-4)

But God, who is rich in mercy, because of His great love with which He loved us, even when we were dead in trespasses, made us alive together with Christ (by grace you have been saved), and raised us up together, and made us sit together in the heavenly places in Christ Jesus, that in the ages to come He might show the exceeding riches of His grace in His kindness toward us in Christ Jesus. (Ephesians 2:4-7)

Blessed be the God and Father of our Lord Jesus Christ, who according to His abundant mercy has begotten us again to a living hope through the resurrection of Jesus Christ from the dead. (1 Peter 1:3)

What if a visiting grandparent had told them stories of God's amazing mercy to His undeserving people? After God delivered the Israelites from Egypt and brought them safely to Mount Sinai, the people made a golden calf and worshipped it while Moses was on the mountain meeting with God. Moses pleaded with God not to abandon them in the desert even though they deserved punishment. To comfort Moses, God gave him a glimpse of His glory as He proclaimed His name: "The LORD, the LORD God, merciful and gracious, longsuffering, and abounding in goodness and truth, keeping mercy for thousands, forgiving iniquity and transgression and sin" (Exodus 34:6-7a).

After David disobeyed God by sleeping with another man's wife, his conscience sorely bothered him. In Psalm 51:1-3, he wrote, "Have mercy upon me, O God, according to Your loving-kindness; according to the multitude of Your tender mercies, blot out my transgressions. Wash me thoroughly from my iniquity, and cleanse me from my sin. For I acknowledge my transgressions, and my sin is always before me." The Lord forgave David because he was sincerely sorry and determined not to repeat his offense. In Psalm 23, David wrote these comforting words: "Surely goodness and mercy shall follow me all the days of my life" (v. 6).

Children need to learn that the throne of God in the temple was called the "mercy seat." The throne room is where a king dispenses justice and mercy to his people. On the Day of Atonement, the high priest of Israel would enter God's presence in the Most Holy Place and ask God's forgiveness for the nation. The gold-covered chest in this special room contained sacred items symbolizing God's merciful dealings with His people in the past: Moses' stone tablets, a jar of manna, and Aaron's rod that budded. These relics reminded them God was gracious and not merely just. They could count on Him to give them what they needed and not what they deserved. Because of Jesus' perfect sacrifice, Christians can come boldly to the throne of grace to "obtain mercy and find grace to help in time of need" (Hebrews 4:16).

CHRIST'S MERCY

Imagine for a minute that the boys who brutalized the thirteen-year-old had a Bible school teacher who taught them about the mercy of Christ. For example, the teacher might have shared Jesus' words from the Sermon on the Mount: "Blessed are the merciful, for they shall obtain mercy" (Matthew 5:7).

Would they have behaved differently had they learned the parable of the prodigal son? In this story, a young man who was disobedient and disrespectful to his father realized he had made a terrible mistake. When he humbled himself and came home, his father ran to greet him and prepared a celebration in honor of his return. It was not what he deserved, but it was what he desperately needed.

Would they have been kinder had they learned the story of the good Samaritan? A man traveling a dangerous road from Jerusalem to Jericho was beaten and robbed. A priest and Levite passed by without helping the injured man, but a Samaritan treated his wounds and arranged for additional care. Jesus asked, "Who was neighbor to the man?" The correct answer was "The one who showed him mercy." Those who please God do not beat others down and mistreat them. They do not bypass others and minimize them. Instead, they build them up by ministering to them.

Sometimes, Jesus told heartwarming stories illustrating the appeal of mercy as a way of life. In other instances, He told shocking stories of coldhearted souls who withheld mercy from those in desperate circumstances. There was the unforgiving elder brother who held a grudge against the prodigal (and his father), refusing to celebrate his brother's return. Then, there was the unfeeling rich man who would not even share the crumbs of his table with the beggar Lazarus, who was only steps away from where he feasted on a daily basis. Yet worst of all was Jesus' unforgettable account of a despicable man known as the unmerciful servant (Matthew 18:21-35).

A man who was in debt up to his eyeballs was called to settle his accounts. Unable to repay the loan, his master commanded that he and his entire family be sold into slavery. But then something marvelous happened. As the servant pleaded for more time to come up with the money, the master was moved with compassion and released him. Knowing his servant could never repay him, he simply forgave the debt. As stunning as it was, a more incredible scene was to follow.

Shortly after his release, the forgiven man set out to find his own creditors to reestablish his finances. Locating one, he grabbed him by the throat, demanding repayment. In a scene eerily similar to the earlier experience, the man fell to his knees, begging for more time. Rather than leniency, he gave the man what the law said he deserved: jail time. However, that was not the end of the story.

When his fellow servants saw his heartlessness, they reported it to the forgiving master, who called him to account for his conduct. The master told him that one who receives pity and pardon is morally if not legally obligated to treat others with similar compassion. In his mind, ingratitude was a far greater crime that misappropriating funds. This transgression would not be overlooked. He would spend the rest of his life in prison for his miscalculation. Today, those who are ungrateful are confined in a prison of their own making.

The master in Jesus' story was a slightly veiled reference to God, who forgives our sins when we ask for mercy. One who receives such a great gift ought to forgive the comparatively minor offenses of others. Jesus said insensitivity to the suffering of others is more than wrong; it makes God downright angry (not a good idea). How much better to delight God and honor Him by sharing what you have received. Jesus urged, "Therefore be merciful, just as your Father also is merciful" (Luke 6:36).

One last thought before leaving this subject: Would the older teens in our story have chosen a different course had they known the story of Jesus on the cross? Jesus did not deserve to die, but wicked men thought He did. They said, "You get what you deserve." They stripped Him of His clothes and nailed Him to a cross to torture and humiliate Him. They did not realize He was God's Son with the power to unleash the army of heaven to punish them. It was what they deserved, but Jesus chose to give them something different: mercy. In His agony, He prayed from the cross, "Father, forgive them, for they know not what they do" (Luke 23:34 ESV). You wonder if they knew that story.

PAUL'S MERCY

Nothing distinguishes God's people like mercy, and aside from the cross, no story better illustrates this point than the conversion of Saul of Tarsus. At one point, he was a promising young Pharisee whose star was on the rise. He mercilessly persecuted Christians, and the zeal that distinguished his career was fired by pure hatred. Breathing out threats and slaughter, he said, "You get what you deserve." Then he met Jesus on the road to Damascus, and everything changed. Receiving forgiveness, he could not deny it to others.

Saul was a new man and devoted the remainder of his life to practicing and proclaiming the mercy of Christ. He explained,

"For this reason I obtained mercy, that in me first Jesus Christ might show all longsuffering, as a pattern to those who are going to believe on Him for everlasting life" (1 Timothy 1:16). In other words, if He can forgive me, He can forgive you. To those who accepted God's mercy, he issued a parallel to Micah's challenge: "Let all bitterness, wrath, anger, clamor, and evil speaking be put away from you, with all malice. And be kind to one another, tenderhearted, forgiving one another, even as God in Christ forgave you" (Ephesians 4:31-32; cf. Micah 6:8). How I wish someone had told those hate-filled teens Saul's inspiring story.

YOUR MERCY

So how will you show your gratitude for God's amazing grace? Christianity is about compassion and not just chasteness. Morality is important, but mercy is a weightier matter in God's eyes. Jude prayed for mercy, peace, and love to be multiplied among those contending for the faith because he knew ruthlessness in opposing error is as unbecoming as it is ineffective (Jude 2). Mercy is the earmark of authentic Christianity.

Sooner than you think, you will open your eyes in eternity, and you will account to God for your treatment of others. On that day, you will be measured relationally (Matthew 25:34-40) as well as morally (Galatians 5:19-21) and doctrinally (John 12:48). James declared, "For judgment is without mercy to the one who has shown no mercy. Mercy triumphs over judgment" (James 2:13).

The truth is, no one deserves mercy (Romans 3:23). That is what makes the gospel such good news. Mercy means you do not get what you deserve. Hallelujah! Instead of eternal punishment, you are promised eternal glory. Rather than weeping and gnashing of teeth, God will wipe away every tear from your eyes. You deserve hell, but you get heaven.

Perhaps Jeremiah put it best: "Through the LORD's mercies we are not consumed, because His compassions fail
not. They are new every morning; great is Your faithfulness"
(Lamentations 3:22-23). Every morning when you get up, thank
God for His mercy and ask Him to help you fill your day with
acts of mercy. Be on the lookout for opportunities to do good
and relieve suffering. No matter what someone says or does, do
not run out of compassion and kindness. Give them what they
need. Not what they deserve.

Mercy

SELF-ASSESSMENT

Y N 1. Do I give people only what they deserve (justice)?

Y N 2. Do I delight in giving people what they need (grace)?

Y N 3. Do I "love" mercy, or do I bestow it begrudgingly?

Y N 4. Do I "walk humbly" with God by recalling His mercy to me?

Y N 5. Do I prefer mercy over judgment?

QUESTIONS

1. What three things does God require (Micah 6:8)?

2. What name did Paul give God in 2 Corinthians 1:3?

3. What did God promise the merciful (Matthew 5:7)?

4. Why did Paul say he obtained mercy (1 Timothy 1:16)?

5. For what did Jude pray (Jude 2)?

DISCUSSION

1. How do people learn mercy?

2. Why do you need to "love" mercy?

3. Why is God's throne called the "mercy seat"?

4. What is the message behind the objects preserved in the ark of the covenant?

5. Why did Jude pray for mercy to abound when battling false teachers?

6. What does mercy have to do with judgment?

7. What is your takeaway from the parable of the unforgiving servant?

8. How are the Lord's mercies new every morning?

EXERCISE

List three ways your congregation (or family) will become more merciful.

1

2

3

AUBREY JOHNSON

CHAPTER 8

Be Hospitable

Open your heart—open it wide; someone is standing outside.

—Mary Engelbreit

When you think of memorials, you may think of statues of heroic figures fashioned from granite or marble. When God chose a memorial, He used a table. Hebrews 9:2 says, "For a tent was prepared, the first section, in which were the lampstand and the table and the bread of Presence. It is called the Holy Place" (ESV). On the left side of the sanctuary sat the lampstand. On the right side was the table of showbread on which rested the bread of presence.

The table was made of acacia wood overlaid with gold to convey its preciousness. The dimensions were three feet long, a foot and a half deep, and two feet three inches tall. On this table were twelve loaves of bread, one for each tribe of Israel. Fresh loaves replaced the old ones each Sabbath day, and the priests, as representatives of the people, ate the week-old bread in the Holy Place. This simple meal symbolized Israel's dependence upon God, who supplied all their needs.

Eating together implies fellowship. Putting a table in the chamber adjoining the Most Holy Place was God's way of saying Israel enjoyed a special relationship with Him. They were near and dear to His heart. The bread was evidence of His commitment to caring for His covenant people. The table's proximity to the ark and unending supply of bread communicated God's undying devotion.

THE PREPARED TABLE

In describing God's love and care for His covenant people, David said, "You prepare a table before me in the presence of my enemies" (Psalm 23:5a). God is always preparing a table for those He loves. Enemies want to take from us, but God wants to give us what we need and more.

Those who are like God also prepare tables for others. Few things reflect a genuine spiritual connection to God better than hospitality. Church leaders who model Christlikeness to the congregation must practice hospitality (1 Timothy 3:2; Titus 1:8). Likewise, faithful Christians must open their hearts and homes to those in need. Welcome guests include fellow saints (Romans 12:13), strangers (Hebrews 13:2), and the sick and poor (Luke 14:13). Hospitality is its own reward, but added blessings will be yours at the resurrection (v. 14). However, one reminder is in order. The hospitality that pleases God must be done without complaint (1 Peter 4:9). Hospitality without love is opportunism (1 Corinthians 13:1-3). It is motivated by guilt or self-interest rather than grace and empathy.

Prepared tables are about fellowship as well as food. Knowing you have a seat waiting for you at a Thanksgiving meal is one of life's greatest joys. In addition to the turkey and pumpkin pie are the warm greetings of family and friends. Special touches like centerpieces and napkin rings convey that someone wants to make you feel loved. Adornments are signs of affection and appreciation.

My wife, Lisa, leaves the table set at all times. Why? So she will never miss a chance to extend hospitality. Many opportunities come up suddenly and unexpectedly. Rather than having to decline because the house is not ready, she can calmly have people over at the drop of a hat. Even when things are not as tidy as she would like, she refuses to let that stand in the way of fellowship. Too often, we worry more about being judged than being gracious. When the goal is to bless others rather than impress them, love finds a way.

MEMORABLE OLD TESTAMENT TABLES

Unlike other rulers who fared sumptuously at the expense of the people, Nehemiah was famous for hosting 150 Jews and rulers at his table every day (Nehemiah 5:17-18). After Jonathan died in battle, his son, Mephibosheth, ate at David's table like one of the king's own sons (2 Samuel 9:11). Just the sight of Solomon's table overwhelmed the queen of Sheba. Its beauty and bounty surpassed all she had previously heard about his greatness (2 Chronicles 9:3-6).

In contrast to Solomon's extravagance was a strikingly simple table provided to Elisha by the Shunammite woman (2 Kings 4:10-12). No doubt, he ate at the table of his benefactor when passing through the area, but in addition to the typical hospitality afforded a traveler, she prepared a private room for the prophet that included a table and chair. It is hard to imagine the pleasure it brought him to know he was welcome and could relax and do his work in comfort. The spartan accommodations were perfect for his needs and did not take away in the least from his enjoyment of them.

NOTEWORTHY NEW TESTAMENT TABLES

The New Testament mentions several tables where Jesus was a guest. Martha was always delighted to have Jesus at her table, though she sometimes struggled with the necessities of hosting the many guests He attracted (Luke 10:38-40). Less enthusiastic was Simon. He invited Jesus to dine with him but doubted He was a prophet since Jesus allowed a disreputable woman to touch Him (7:36-40). Jesus pointed out the difference between Simon's cool reception and the sinful woman's lavish displays of devotion. She was beholden to Jesus because she knew her sinfulness and His power to forgive sin. Simon was unimpressed by Jesus because he trusted in his own righteousness and doubted his guest was more than a common man. Jesus ended with an idea for Simon to chew on after dinner was over: "He who is forgiven little, loves little" (Luke 7:47 ESV). The table is a great place for learning as well as for bonding and feeding the body. It is a place to teach manners and impart lessons for abundant living. Mealtime is sacred time when used as God intended.

One day, Jesus was invited to recline at the table of a Pharisee who was deeply bothered when Jesus did not go through the usual ceremonial washing before the meal (Luke 11:37-40). Unknown to His host, Jesus deliberately "set the table" for the discussion that followed. The Pharisee obsessed about external washings but did not give the same attention to purifying his heart. Jesus said his practice was as silly as someone washing the outside of cups and bowls and putting them away for the next meal. The image is as repulsive as it is ridiculous, but that is precisely what many do as vessels of God.

Hygienically speaking, if you could wash only one part, would it not be better to wash the inside? Pharisees were scrupulous in keeping their traditions but less painstaking in caring for their neighbors. Their primary concern was their image, not their fellow man. Justice and mercy spring from a pure heart. It is about blessing you rather than impressing you. So how clean is your cup? Do not be fooled by its shiny appearance as it sits high on a shelf. Pull it down, look closer, peer inside. A little more soap, please?

When lawyers in attendance protested that Jesus insulted them, He did not give an inch. Instead, He took the conversation even deeper by pronouncing woes upon them should they continue their current behavior. Jesus provided specific examples of their wrongdoing to urge them to repent. On some occasions, table talk can provide accountability for those who need a better grasp on reality. Backing down from difficult conversations does not serve those we love. Nagging is counterproductive, but honesty provides food for thought when it is timely and motivated by genuine interest in the other's well-being.

THE UNUSED TABLE

A prepared table is a beautiful thing in God's eyes. In contrast, an overturned table is a pitiful sight to behold (Matthew 21:12), and a misused table is its own kind of tragedy (2 John 7-11; 1 Corinthians 10:21; 1 Kings 18:19). Yet the saddest table of all is an empty table. In the parable of the wedding feast, Jesus described one of the most sorrowful scenes in the Bible: the tale of the empty table.

> And again Jesus spoke to them in parables, saying, "The kingdom of heaven may be compared to a king who gave a wedding feast for his son, and sent his servants to call those who were invited to the wedding feast, but they would not come." (Matthew 22:1-3 ESV)

The setting of the story is a time of supreme joy. A father is preparing a celebration for the wedding of his son. The host is king of the realm, and his son, the prince. The food has been carefully prepared by a skillful chef. Choice beef and oxen are on the menu. The table has been set and decorated for the honored guests. Everything is ready. Invitations were extended, and now the servants are sent out to notify everyone on the guest list that the feast is ready.

There is only one problem. No one comes. Assuming there has been some misunderstanding, the host sends out more servants. "Tell those who are invited, 'See, I have prepared my dinner, my oxen and my fat calves have been slaughtered, and everything is ready. Come to the wedding feast'" (Matthew 22:4 ESV). Still, the table sat empty.

What was the problem? Not dereliction of duty by the servants. Not miscommunication. The guests simply declined to come. They went about their daily affairs as if nothing special was happening. They overlooked the magnitude of the occasion and the honor of the invitation. Consequently, they insulted the host and proved themselves unworthy of his generosity. The empty table was a reflection of their empty hearts.

THE EMPTY SEAT

Almost as sad as an empty table is an empty seat that should be filled. Judas enjoyed a place at the table of Jesus and His apostles, but one day his spot went unfilled. "For," said Peter, "it is written in the Book of Psalms: 'May his place be deserted; let there be no one to dwell in it'" (Acts 1:20 NIV). When Judas betrayed Jesus, he gave up his place at the table of the Lord.

But the problem is not always with the guest. You remember that the king was concerned the servants might not have fulfilled their duty. He sent out different servants to make sure his message was received. In the church, we are the servants who call others to take a place of honor around the table of the Lord. Jesus is the Prince, and His Father, the King, bids all to come to the wedding feast. Through evangelism and hospitality, we do our part to furnish the wedding with guests.

The danger is we may become so concerned with our own place at the table that we forget our sacred duty. Think of the rich man who denied Lazarus a place at his table only to lose his own seat at Abraham's bosom (Luke 16:19-25). Recall the angry older brother who would deny his younger brother a place at his father's table (15:25-28). Or consider the Pharisee whose chief concern was securing a place of honor for himself (14:7).

Jesus would have His servants "go therefore to the main roads and invite to the wedding feast as many as you find" (Matthew 22:9 ESV). We cannot be preoccupied like the rich man, self-absorbed like the Pharisee, or self-righteous like the older brother. Our calling is clear: let us fill every possible seat at the table. When we do, the King is pleased, the Son is honored, the guests are blessed, and our enjoyment of the feast is multiplied by the fellowship of those who join us there.

Inviting people to services is a good way to introduce them to Jesus, but we must also make them feel welcome once they arrive. Verbal greetings are valuable, but silent greetings are also desirable. Consider one silent signal you can send to let people know you are glad they are there.

THE EMPTY PEW

When you were a kid, did you hate being at the end of the line? When fixing sandwiches, did you give your brother the ends of the loaf? Most people do not like ends, but there is one exception—everyone loves the end of the pew. Some camp on the end of the pew for the comfort of an armrest. Others do it for better visibility. The impatient are looking for a quick escape. Longtime members consider it a cherished right to be defended. As a result, lots of real estate goes unused in the middle of the pew.

Now, imagine you are a visitor to your services. Suppose you are a little shy and feel anxious in new surroundings. You want to check out the congregation because you heard good things about it. Still, you don't like attention and prefer to be inconspicuous. Arriving minutes early, you scan the auditorium for easy access to a pew. To your distress, every end seat is filled. While you delay, the announcements begin, and everyone's attention is front and center. Halfway down the center aisle, you see enough room for your family of four. When you approach, the couple on the end of the row looks up a little startled. Rather than scooting down, they shift their legs, allowing you inches to pass. The whole congregation watches as you slide in awkwardly and bump your knee, first on a songbook rack and then on a woman's knee.

The service was fine, but you were so mortified by your grand entrance that it took a while to refocus on worship. It cooled your enthusiasm and colored your impression of everything that happened the rest of the morning. Folks were friendly after service, but the memory of those first few moments lingers in your mind. The next Sunday morning, you wake up late, and everyone is rushed. You know you will be a few minutes behind for service, but skipping is not an option. When your spouse asks, "Where do you want to worship today?", the first thing you remember is the embarrassment you felt last week. Unable to bear a repeat, you opt for a different congregation.

When guests come to your house, do you take the comfy couch and offer them stiff ladder-back chairs? If you give visitors the best seats in your house, why not give visitors the best seats in God's house? *Are you serious? Leave the ends of the pews for visitors?* Absolutely! For all the reasons you enjoy an end seat, so will they. Imagine a church where the ends of the pews are unoccupied, as if they were expecting company. To paraphrase a line from a movie, "If you leave it, they will come." Why not let God fill the ends of our pews?

America's sparsely populated heartland has often been referred to as "flyover states." It is easy to overlook states like Oklahoma and Kansas in favor of densely populated ones like California and New York. Though coastal cities have attracted more people than mid-America, there is something special about the ignored central states. Like thinly inhabited parts of the country, the middle of a church pew is less favored territory than an aisle seat. My hope is we will not overlook the preciousness of an interior pew. I want church members everywhere to stop living on the edge: the edge of the pew that is. Don't hang on to your favorite seat like a stubborn squatter or entitled owner. Give a little love to a middle seat and spread the love of Jesus.

To create the most welcoming culture possible, it takes more than good intentions: it takes deliberate practice. The Golden Rule asks you to do unto others as you would have them do unto you. So imagine you approach a pew and are prepared to squeeze by its gatekeeper. When you get his attention, he looks up at you, greets you with a smile, and scoots to the middle. How would that make you feel? Even better, imagine entering a packed church auditorium, yet you see aisle seats in abundance. How would that make you feel, and what would it tell you about the congregation?

When you see all that open real estate in the center of a pew, realize it is an opportunity to grow spiritually and to bless an anxious visitor. The gospel challenge is to be so focused on others that it shows in all you do: even where you sit. To be considerate, by all means be hospitable.

THE BEST TABLE

Of all the tables mentioned in the Bible, the most precious is the table of the Lord. The Lord's Table epitomizes everything it means to be a Christian. It is feast and fellowship on a grand spiritual scale. It is also a weekly touchstone with God's call to live a considerate life by thinking of others more than yourself. The Lord's Table does this by memorializing the sacrificial life of Jesus on behalf of those He loves. He came for us, saved us, and now hosts us until He returns for us. In the meantime, He models for us the best of all possible lives: a life where those who follow in His footsteps consider one another.

Hospitality

SELF-ASSESSMENT

Y   N   1. Do I open my home to newcomers in the congregation or neighborhood?

Y   N   2. Do I open my home to church members with whom I am unfamiliar?

Y   N   3. Do I open my home to widows, the poor, or the church's youth (those outside my circle)?

Y   N   4. Do I practice hospitality without complaint?

Y   N   5. Do I show hospitality to visitors at church assemblies?

QUESTIONS

1. What table did God use as a memorial in the temple (Hebrews 9:2)?

2. What did God prepare for David in the presence of his enemies (Psalm 23:5)?

3. Who prepared a table for Elisha (2 Kings 4:12)?

4. How many Jews and rulers did Nehemiah host at his expense every day (Nehemiah 5:17-18)?

5. Who was impressed by the magnificence of Solomon's table (2 Chronicles 9:3-6)?

DISCUSSION

1. What was God saying by placing a table in the temple?

2. What was the significance of the location of the table of showbread?

3. Why did God command church leaders to practice hospitality?

4. How do you think Elisha felt when a woman prepared him a room with a table?

5. How precious is it to have a place around the table with family at Thanksgiving?

6. What do table adornments say to guests? What are some of your favorites?

7. What does leaving seats at the ends of pews communicate to guests?

8. How precious is it to know you have a place at the Lord's Table each Sunday?

EXERCISE

List three ways your congregation (or family) will become more hospitable.

1

2

3

CHAPTER 9
Be Understanding

Sometimes someone says something really small,
and it just fits right into this empty place in your heart.

—My So-Called Life

I am so glad God does not hold grudges. Can you imagine what life would be like under an infinite God who was irritable, unapproachable, and impossible to please? Psalm 86:5 says, "For you, O Lord, are good and forgiving, abounding in steadfast love to all who call upon you" (ESV). What could be more comforting? Then again, what could be more challenging? When you become a Christian, you are called not only to forgiveness but also to holiness. In other words, you are called to be more like God with each passing day. So, instead of nursing grudges, you must be willing—even eager—to put the past behind you. You must stop resenting.

A DEFINITION
The word "resent" comes from the prefix "re," expressing intensity, and the French word *sentir*, which means to feel. Resentment is a powerful negative emotion toward those you believe have mistreated you. Resentment stirs bitter feelings, drives people apart, causes ill will, and may spark vengeance. When you are resentful, you feel aggrieved, but you also feel annoyed when something good happens to the person you think injured you.

A CHALLENGE

To stop resenting is no easy task. To stop resenting, *you* must cease doing *it*. *It* must come to an end, but that does not happen apart from *you*. Many people are waiting for another person to apologize and make amends before they will give up brooding and fuming. The problem is waiting on others places your emotional well-being at their disposal. Talk about slavery. The good news is Christians can abandon resentment at any time regardless of what others may do. The truth that sets you free is resentment is a choice.

A MOTIVATION

When you choose not to move on when someone frustrates, disappoints, or hurts you, what are the consequences? Emotionally, it traps you in negativity, robbing you of peace and joy and pulling you down to new lows. You make a habit of collecting and storing grievances real and imagined. Your soul is transformed into a cluttered closet packed full of useless memories from your past. Resentment feeds on itself and grows. Physically, it compromises your health. When you feel depressed, you may sleep fitfully and feel fatigued in the morning. You are less likely to exercise and eat well compared to days when you are feeling upbeat. Professionally, you find it hard to concentrate and do your job. Just getting through the day can be difficult. Socially, people avoid you lest your gloomy spirit infect them and bring them down too. Worst of all, the spiritual consequences of resentment are stagnation or regression. Rather than advancing in Christlikeness, you begin to retreat. Instead of walking by the Spirit, you wallow in the flesh. To habitually resent others is to return to a less spiritual, less healthy, and less enjoyable state. You are stuck in a past you cannot change.

CAUSES

What is the source of resentment in relationships? A careless word, broken promise, or thoughtless act. No sleight was intended, but you took exception nonetheless. Frustration led to judgment and then to condemnation. Motives were assumed and impugned. You say words such as "you should have" or "shouldn't have," indicating your expectations were reasonable but unmet. But the presenting problem is seldom the true cause of failed friendships. The main culprit is sin. Selfishness is the driving force behind grudges and life's un-get-overable incidents.

Often, the disappointment is directed at those closest to you: a spouse, child, parent, friend, boss, coworker, or fellow Christian. Why? Because you spend more time around them, you have more opportunities to find grievances and build resentment. The more history you have with someone, the more irritations can mount.

EXAMPLES

The Bible is filled with stories of people who harbored resentment to their own detriment. Cain loathed Abel because he was jealous of the approval his obedient brother received from God. Sarah despised Hagar even though the love triangle threatening her marriage was of her own making. Satan hated Job for maintaining his integrity and refusing to blaspheme God. Korah resented Moses because he projected his ambition onto a meek man who reluctantly accepted God's call. Ahab detested Elijah and blamed the prophet for the drought caused by his own sins. Haman's irrational envy of Mordecai led to his own death on the very gallows he built for his self-made enemy. Herod was so self-absorbed that he disliked newborn babies who might pose a threat to his power one day.

SOLUTIONS

The problem with resentment is it filters everything through the lens of self-interest and then places the responsibility for resolution on the other person. Consequently, everything is out of your hands. You are a passive participant in the negative events happening to you. Resentment is choosing the role of the victim. The solution is to take a more active role in your life. The answer is more personal accountability. You must choose a new part in this drama: the role of the responsible man or woman. Everything begins to change for the better when you decide to create a new and better future.

Solution #1: Desire—You Have to Want It

Desire is the key to defeating resentment. It is hard to get over a grudge if you feel it is reasonable and justified. Rather than resolving differences, you bask in your superiority. But ask yourself a question: "How is that resentment working for you?" How much better to envision the outcome you want rather than to stroke your hurt ego. Resentment is a choice that becomes a habit that turns into an addiction. For some, the pain becomes their identity. Rehearsing past offenses and the reasons you are "right" changes nothing. It merely drives the story deeper into your heart. The way forward is not to deny hurt feelings and stuff them. The answer is to process them. How? Through more understanding. But everything begins with a strong desire for things to be different—so strong, in fact, that you are willing to take the first step.

Solution #2: Understanding—You Have to Frame It

Understand the real source of resentment may reside within you and the way you are framing events. Understand someone may be having a bad day and you took it personally. Understand you are not perfect and may have contributed to the problem (could it be that you need to apologize?). Understand people, the spiritual roots of unhappiness, and the options before you. Most of all, you need to understand your own heart. What is needed to overcome resentment? More humility, honesty, and sympathy. Understanding makes it easier to forbear and forgive. It shifts your heart into reconciliation mode. The result is more patience, kindness, and gratitude. Equipped with new insight, you are ready to courageously blaze a trail forward.

Understanding lets you appreciate imperfect people. A heart full of gratitude has little room for grudges. The instant ill feelings begin to rise, make a list of things you are thankful for about the person or situation upsetting you. Ahab, one of the wealthiest men in Israel, resented Naboth for not selling him the vineyard passed down through his family. Eve, surrounded by the beauty and bounty of Eden, resented that she could not eat from one solitary tree. Discontent is a byproduct of ingratitude. It is fixating on what displeases you to the exclusion of what delights you. Resentment blurs your vision and clouds your perspective due to a preoccupation with your rights, needs, and desires.

Solution #3: Prayer—You Have to Release It

When you focus on your grievances, it is hard to appreciate anyone or anything. The older brother begrudged the prodigal's homecoming party and his place in the family. Why? Because he focused on the inconvenience his brother caused him. He assumed the worst about his brother rather than the best. The more you assume motives, the deeper your resentment goes, but you do it to yourself. Rather than believing the best, you choose to doubt the other's sincerity and disregard his efforts to make things right. The older brother would not budge. He was unwilling to make the slightest effort to welcome or comfort his sorrowful sibling. He did not frame it like his father because he did not want restoration. Consequently, he clung to his grievance and nursed his grudge.

When the father saw his son returning, his response was just the opposite. He did not withdraw or coolly wait for him to approach and grovel. He ran to him, and get this, he met him more than halfway. Why? Because his heart was full of joy rather than resentment. Consequently, the future would be brighter sooner. Hebrews says, "Let us also lay aside every weight, and sin which clings so closely, and let us run with endurance the race that is set before us" (12:1b ESV). Why is it important to forgive others? So we can "run" (Isaiah 40:31). The father chose to lay aside his wounded pride for the sake of his family. He chose love and was willing to throw off the thoughts and emotions that would have hindered healing his home.

One purpose of prayer is to release your pain and cast it upon Christ, who deeply cares when you are hurting. If you can't fix it, just let it go. Why carry it around? Leave the outcome to Him. That is what the cross is all about. Resentment is a weight around your soul. Leave it at the cross, where Jesus suffered and died to remove all the sin of all the broken relationships in all the world throughout all of history! That is the power of prayer. That is the power of the cross. So why would anyone cling to resentment one second longer?

The parable of the prodigal son is more than a story. Jesus wanted you to know that ridding your life of resentment is a real possibility. You can choose a new future. Instead of spending your time in sadness and regret, imagine better days—then create them! How? Bless those who speak ill of you. Pray for those who hurt you. Do good to those who disappoint you. Do not waste another minute in anger. With each kind word, prayer, and deed, you reverse the effects of sin. Negative emotions that injure you and isolate you will dissipate. In their place, sow seeds of grace and goodwill that will produce a harvest of righteousness. When you think loving thoughts, say loving words, and do loving deeds, resentment cannot grow in your heart.

CONCLUSION

The solution to strained relationships is not to linger on the past or to constantly litigate your case against others. The answer is to send some love their way. Instead of retreating, run to meet them. Rather than retaliating, do them a kindness. In other words, the way forward is to become more like Christ. Do not be peevish or impatient. Do not be easily offended and vindictive. Do not be crabby or cross. The key is for you to grow rather than wait on others to change.

Relational difficulties are bound to occur, yet relationships do not have to remain troubled. The key is to believe things can improve (faith) and to begin making better choices (repentance). Envision how things will improve when you grow past your differences by putting biblical solutions to work in your life. Reaching up to God for help and reaching out to others in hope is heaven's answer for what ails you.

Understanding

SELF-ASSESSMENT

Y   N   1. Do I harbor resentment toward someone?

Y   N   2. Do I want to put the past behind me, or do I prefer to nurse my grudge?

Y   N   3. Do I believe it is possible to get over grudges with God's help?

Y   N   4. Do I understand that overcoming resentment is a choice?

Y   N   5. Do I bless, pray for, and do good to those who have hurt me?

QUESTIONS

1. What are three attributes of God mentioned in Psalm 86:5?

2. Why do we need to throw off sin (Hebrews 12:1)?

3. What should you do with cares that weigh down your heart (1 Peter 5:7)?

4. What never ceases (Lamentations 3:22-23 ESV)?

5. Who resented Naboth for not selling his family vineyard (1 Kings 21)?

DISCUSSION

1. What is resentment?

2. What causes resentment?

3. What are some effects of resentment?

4. How does resentment make you feel?

5. Why would anyone hold on to a grudge?

6. How can resentment become a habit?

7. Why is it so hard to stop resenting?

8. How do you stop resenting?

EXERCISE

List three ways your congregation (or family) will become more understanding.

1

2

3

AUBREY JOHNSON

CHAPTER 10
Be Responsible

Don't be yourself. Be someone a little nicer.

—Mignon McLaughlin

When you hear the word "responsibility," how does it make you feel? For many people, the reaction is negative. They equate responsibility with struggle, sacrifice, and scrutiny (Romans 12:1; 1 Corinthians 9:27). A more mature person considers the long-term benefits of living responsibly. The things you want most in life are by-products of discipline and diligence. Success and stability are not accidents. They are the predictable outcomes of holding yourself accountable to God. When you honor His values and obey His commands, you are living responsibly. It is a blessed life and not a boring or burdensome one. Conversely, the temporary pleasure of irresponsibility turns to pain and regret every time.

RESPONSIBILITY AND SPIRITUALITY

Jesus said, "All authority has been given to Me in heaven and on earth" (Matthew 28:18). Consequently, Jesus gave many commands that grew out of His love and wisdom. His followers are both obligated and overjoyed to observe each one (vv. 19-20). Obedience is a delight rather than drudgery because Jesus' commands are both reasonable and beneficial (Romans 12:1-2). His rules are improvements, not inconveniences.

Throughout the Gospels, Jesus called His followers to live with increased responsibility.

> For everyone to whom much is given, from him much will be required; and to whom much has been committed, of him they will ask the more. (Luke 12:48)

> For to everyone who has, more will be given, and he will have abundance; but from him who does not have, even what he has will be taken away. (Matthew 25:29)

The apostles issued similar pleas to embrace the responsibilities of discipleship. Paul gave two essentials for living responsibly: do not wrong others (Romans 13:10), and do good to all (Galatians 6:10). He also reminded Christians they are responsible for using their God-given gifts in a Christlike manner (Romans 12:6-13). Diligence in doing good is critical, but the accompanying attitude is equally important. Christians are to be loving, cheerful, and fervent as they go about God's business.

Similarly, Peter issued an urgent plea for diligence in Christian living (2 Peter 1:5-11). Entrance into the everlasting kingdom is conditioned on doing these things. God's desire is for you to add to your present virtues rather than slack off and slip backward. This farsightedness is essential to promote fruitfulness and prevent barrenness.

THE AGE OF ME

Contrary to these biblical mandates, American sensibilities hold that individualism and self-expression are life's supreme virtues. In truth, being responsible does not make you less authentic, creative, or free. Responsible people make civilizations and organizations work. Nonetheless, the media specializes in glamorizing the irresponsible. Those who break rules and defy conventional morals are idolized in pop culture. However, being cool or flamboyant adds little value to society.

Aside from those who are immature due to youth, irresponsible people fall into two categories: those who deny responsibility and those who dodge it. Regardless of the cause, irresponsibility has a negative effect on the individual and those around him. According to the 80-20 rule, only one out of five people is living a highly responsible life. Of the remainder, many are minimalists and mavericks. The former do the least possible to get by, and the latter defy authority for the sheer joy of it. A person who evades responsibility is shifting his obligations to others. Consequently, others must carry more than their fair share of the load.

Responsibility is essential for any person to please God and have a positive experience of life. The question every person must answer is whether a life devoted to pleasure is more joyful and satisfying than a responsible life. Are amusement and self-indulgence preferable to fruitfulness and kindness?

Yet it is not enough to live responsibly. Jesus' followers must also live graciously. Christianity is not just about pulling your weight (Galatians 6:5) but bearing the burdens of others (v. 2). To illustrate this point, let us recall one of Jesus' best-loved parables.

THE SAD STORY OF THE RESPONSIBLE SON

In the parable of the prodigal son, Jesus told the emotional story of a father and his two sons as the boys were coming of age. The youngest son was immature and irresponsible. He thought only of himself and the moment. As a result, he broke his father's heart, disgraced himself, and lost his inheritance.

The good news is he learned something in the process. Broke and starving, he began to reflect on his options. How did he get here, and where could he go from here? He realized he created his situation through a series of selfish choices. He could stay where he was and prolong the pain (the proud thing to do), or he could go home and end the suffering (the humble thing to do). No doubt, it would be embarrassing to admit he was wrong, but that brief moment of discomfort would quickly fade and make room for a whole new set of possibilities. The only thing standing between him and a better future was stubborn pride, so he left his inflated ego in the muck of the pigpen where it belonged.

Upon arriving home, he was unprepared for the enthusiastic reception he received from his father. Rather than waiting for him to grovel, his dad ran to embrace him and immediately began preparations for a homecoming party. But while his father was rejoicing, his older brother was sulking and refused to participate in the festivities. He was angry because he thought an injustice had been done to him. His father had not wronged him, but his thoughts were so full of himself that it felt that way. A kindness to another can feel like a slap in the face to the self-absorbed (Matthew 20:9-13). His father was not condoning or encouraging his brother's irresponsibility. Rather, he was delighting in his deliverance from a destructive lifestyle. His wayward son's humility marked a spiritual turning point worthy of celebration.

Although we usually make the younger son the focal point of the story, Jesus was more concerned with his brooding brother. Down in the dumps, he not only boycotted the party but berated his father for giving it. He had toed the line all his life, and now his father was rewarding his rebel brother who had wasted his wealth and disgraced the family name. No doubt, the prodigal was guilty of irresponsibility, but his dependable brother failed to see he was guilty of another sin: ungraciousness.

Irresponsibility is largely a result of two things: thinking of yourself without considering others and thinking of the present without considering long-term consequences. Responsible people anticipate the probable outcomes of their actions with special concern for the way their decisions impact others. They think cause and effect or, as Paul put it, sowing and reaping. Irresponsible people have a disconnect between the pain they cause and the choices they make. Unrealistic, distorted, selfish thinking is the root of this sin.

Churlishness ignores the needs and feelings of others. Like irresponsibility, it can also be traced to shortsightedness. One is the product of selfishness, and the other, a result of self-righteousness. Sullenly withholding forgiveness is short-sighted because all stand in need of God's mercy. Judgment is without mercy to those who show no mercy (James 2:13).

As the weeks passed and the former prodigal was no longer starving and broke, you cannot help but wonder how his experience changed him. In my mind, he went from sighing "I cannot believe I have to do this" to "I cannot believe I get to do this!" His duties were the same as before, but something was different. He was no longer miserable. Gratitude transformed the mundane tasks of ordinary life into moments to be treasured. He felt blessed rather than shortchanged.

When he asked for his inheritance, he was not ready to handle it. He now realized his father was not holding out on him. He was protecting him rather than punishing him. The point of the parable is that responsibility to God is about your attitude as well as your actions. Make no mistake, it is important to do the right things but also to do them for the right reasons. God is concerned with your frame of mind and not just your fruits (John 15:1-2).

God has requirements, and man has responsibilities
(Micah 6:8). Those responsibilities include just treatment of
your fellow man, mercy for those who fall short of life's demands,
and humility toward God. In the earlier story, the father was
just, merciful, and humble. The tension in the story resulted
from a deficiency of these virtues in the two sons. The prodigal
was irresponsible, insensitive, and arrogant, but when he humbled himself, everything in his life changed for the better. The
older brother was highly responsible but pitiless and pompous.
Unwilling to humble himself, he not only hurt his family, but he
also doomed himself to a life of anger and resentment. No matter
how much money he accumulated in his lifetime, he deprived
himself of earth's greatest treasure: loving relationships.

DRAMA OR DISCIPLESHIP?

The Christian life has more to do with the mundane than
the magnificent, at least as far as the world views it. Actually,
when someone is doing what they ought to do in a responsible way, it is quite spectacular because it is so rare. Living an
honorable, useful, faithful life is preferable to a life of erratic
emotional highs.

Spirituality is not all emotion and hype. Rather, it is about
living responsibly and graciously at the same time. It is about
making sure your words and deeds honor God and bless others.
That does not mean selling all your possessions, although some
do. It does not mean leaving your job and family to become
a missionary, although some will. The fact is it takes a lot of
responsible people to support the missionaries and ministries
of the church. Your life makes their lives possible. The heroes of
the church are people who glorify God in their workplaces and
carry the gospel into their schools. They sacrificially give and

serve in the local church. They live faithful lives within the fabric of society.

What good are rapturous moments if there is no stable church in which to bring people? True spirituality is about newness of life rather than novelty. The church of the first century was not a protest movement or a subversive political group. They prayed for worldly leaders and worked within flawed governments to bring about spiritual change from the inside. Gentle persuasion rather than violence and coercion was the tool of the apostles and early Christians. Christianity is more of a personal revolution than a political one. Paul's ideal of Christian living for the average church member was something he called the quiet life (1 Thessalonians 4:11; 1 Timothy 2:2). It is about bearing your own load and assuming your own responsibility (Galatians 6:5).

RESPONSIBILITY AND ETERNITY

Responsibility involves an obligation. Christians are responsible to other people but especially to God. The judgment is a day of accounting for your responsibilities. Speaking to the unbelieving and irresponsible, Paul declared,

> Truly, these times of ignorance God overlooked, but now commands all men everywhere to repent, because He has appointed a day on which He will judge the world in righteousness by the Man whom He has ordained. He has given assurance of this to all by raising Him from the dead. (Acts 17:30-31)

God is gracious to forgive the shortcomings of those who strive to please Him, but He will hold the reckless accountable for their neglect. According to Revelation 2:23, judgment is according to your works and not merely your words. Or as Jesus put it, "Not everyone who says to Me, 'Lord, Lord,' shall enter the kingdom of heaven, but he who does the will of My Father in heaven" (Matthew 7:21). Actions trump empty promises every time.

Righteousness and responsibility go hand in hand. You cannot have one without the other. Good works do not win God's love, but they do win His approval. Responsible living cannot earn your salvation, but it can make your calling and election sure. Heaven will be the home of those who love like Jesus. Love is the foundation of all responsible living. Love compels you to rise above selfishness and scheming. Paul said to owe no man anything but to love one another (Romans 13:8). Love is the essential and never-ending responsibility of those created in God's image.

Responsibility

SELF-ASSESSMENT

Y N 1. Do I react positively or negatively to the word "responsibility"?

Y N 2. Do I view Jesus' commands as reasonable and beneficial?

Y N 3. Do I assume my own responsibilities?

Y N 4. Do I avoid wronging others?

Y N 5. Do I bear others' burdens in addition to pulling my own weight?

QUESTIONS

1. From whom will much be required (Luke 12:48)?

2. What does God do with every branch that bears fruit (John 15:1-2)?

3. What must Christians bear according to Galatians 6:2?

4. What must Christians bear according to Galatians 6:5?

5. Judgment is without mercy to whom (James 2:13)?

DISCUSSION

1. Why do some people view responsibility as boring and burdensome?

2. Why does irresponsibility turn to pain and regret?

3. What does judgment day have to do with responsibility?

4. How is love the foundation of all responsible living?

5. Why do responsible Christians aspire to live quietly?

6. Why is humility the key to living a life of justice and mercy?

7. Does being responsible make you less authentic, creative, or free?

8. Why must Christians live graciously as well as responsibly?

EXERCISE

List three ways your congregation (or family) will become more responsible.

1

2

3

CHAPTER 11
Be Positive

Love me when I least deserve it, because
that's when I really need it.

—Swedish Proverb

Man who is born of woman is of few days and full of trouble"
(Job 14:1). No one knew the truth of these words better than Job.
Troubles are not just for the ignorant and the immoral. Problems
come to the spiritual and the successful. The question is, "How
will you handle them?"

Problems are like waves slapping at the seashore: normal
and constant. Honestly, have you ever had a day without one?
Strangely, many people are shocked and frustrated when problems occur. So how do you deal with the steady flow of challenges
life sends your way? Job responded by trusting God. No matter
what happened, he kept believing, hoping, and loving.

Positive people handle life's ups and downs better than those
trapped in negativity. Pessimism takes a heavy toll on you and
on the people around you. When you are gloomy, you are not at
your best. You lose your balance and focus. You become more
critical and disapproving. You may withdraw or grow combative.
Therefore, to navigate problems safely, to preserve your good
nature, and to safeguard those you love, adopt a positive outlook on life.

EXPECT PROBLEMS

Peter said, "Beloved, do not be surprised at the fiery trial when it comes upon you to test you, as though something strange were happening to you" (1 Peter 4:12 ESV). Problems are not unusual or unpredictable. Wise people know a new one is coming around the bend at any moment. Do not be shocked. Instead, be ready to remain steady.

The key is to expect the unexpected. Unrealistic expectations rob you of more joy than circumstances themselves. In most cases, attitude determines life experience. Do you dread problems or look at them as moments of discovery? Negative expectations have a way of becoming self-fulfilling prophecies. If you think "this is going to be bad," you are probably right. If you think "this is going to be interesting," you are probably right. Positive attitudes turn unwanted experiences into times of learning, loving, and sometimes laughing.

INSPECT PROBLEMS

To "inspect" something means to look at it closely to assess its true nature or condition. When you look at problems a little closer, you see things others overlook. For example, the greater the problem, the greater your growth prospects. Any trial can make you a better person, but it must change you in the process (James 1:3-4). Beneficial change is more likely to occur when you are in a positive frame of mind and when you are around others with an optimistic outlook. That is what friendship, fellowship, and family were intended to provide. Choose to spend more time with hopeful and helpful people, and purpose to be someone who blesses rather than burdens others.

James said, "Count it all joy, my brothers, when you meet trials of various kinds" (James 1:2 ESV). Though problems are not painless, neither are they pointless. James believed Christians should be thankful for occasions to grow and glorify God. Problems produce a special kind of pleasure—not worldly enjoyment, but the satisfaction that comes from spiritual insight and growth. The amazing thing is this pleasing perspective is possible whatever the trial may be. Count it "all" joy. Trials come in various forms and sizes. There are big ones and little ones, nuisances and heartbreakers. However undesirable a problem may seem, God always brings good out of evil for those who love Him (Romans 8:28).

CORRECT PROBLEMS

The gospel is the power of God to counteract sin's troublesome consequences. Power is force or energy to effect change. What kind of change did Paul have in mind? The gospel is divine power for salvation and sanctification. Forgiveness and fruitful living require contact with God's Word and those in whom His Word dwells. You are His point of contact for recharging faith-depleted souls. So how do people feel after spending time with you? More empowered or less? Are you a spiritual charging station or a drain on their emotional reserves?

In writing to the troubled Corinthians, Paul shared three traits that would change their futures for the better: faith, hope, and love (1 Corinthians 13:13). These indispensable virtues have a special quality about them: they "abide." That means they have a proven track record of success. You can count on them to work in the most difficult of times. These qualities are potent problem solvers and powerful influence multipliers. In short, they help you live a more considerate life. How? Let's take a look.

Positive People Are People of Faith

Faith in God is transformational. Jesus said, "Do not let your hearts be troubled. You believe in God; believe also in me"

(John 14:1 NIV). Faith turns troubled people into trusting people. How do you face an uncertain future? How do you cope with loss? How do you recover and reengage life? Faith makes the seemingly impossible surpassingly possible. When you are sick, faith gives you courage. When you are sad, faith gives you comfort. When you are stressed, faith gives you composure. To enjoy life more, trust more.

Trust is the path to inner peace. Paul said, "Do not be anxious about anything, but in everything by prayer and supplication with thanksgiving let your requests be made known to God. And the peace of God, which surpasses all understanding, will guard your hearts and your minds in Christ Jesus" (Philippians 4:6-7 ESV). Faith is equal to "anything" you come up against. Anxious hearts become peaceful hearts through believing prayer. Peace of this kind is beyond human comprehension. It requires you to trust that God is doing good even when you do not understand His timetable or plan (Isaiah 55:9). Faith and anxiousness cannot coexist.

Trust dispels fear, but the opposite is also true: no faith, no peace. You are not smart enough or strong enough to fix every problem on your own. It is time you stopped bearing the weight of the world on your shoulders. It is time you let God have a turn running the universe. Faith relieves you of responsibility you were never designed to handle. When you let God take His rightful place, you feel the peace return.

Faith in others is inspirational. It lifts your spirit in an otherwise disheartening world. Imagine what the world would be like if you believed the best about others rather than expecting the worst. Paul said love believes all things (1 Corinthians 13:7). You don't have to be naive to assume positive intent on the part of others. Yes, you will occasionally be disappointed, but not nearly as often as you think. Faith in others brings out their best.

AUBREY JOHNSON

It is a better way to live, and it makes the world a better place in which to live.

When you judge and resent others, your anger creates a barrier and a backlash (Luke 6:37-38). It turns friends into foes and colleagues into combatants. Not everyone will live up to your expectations, but perhaps your expectations are unreasonable. Perhaps it would be better to accept people as they are while encouraging them to do better. Do not postpone happiness until they change to suit you. No one is perfect, including you, but faith draws out untapped potential in ways cynicism never will. The faith of a wife may change her husband over forty years of marriage (1 Peter 3:1-4). The faith of a mother may transform her teenage son over a decade (or two) of prayer, teaching, and encouragement (Proverbs 22:6).

Faith in yourself is motivational. Okay, so you've had some missteps along the way. Do not stop believing in yourself. You are lovable, valuable, and capable. You were created in God's image and filled with incredible potential for good. Peter said, "Grow in the grace and knowledge of our Lord and Savior Jesus Christ" (2 Peter 3:18). God would not demand something you cannot do. God engineered you for success. You can change. You can improve. With faith, nothing is impossible. The key is not self-sufficiency. The way forward is to believe you are equipped by God to accomplish His will (Hebrews 13:20-21). Faith is not pride or arrogance. It is trust and humility. This is where positive change begins. This is the power of faith.

Positive People Are People of Hope

Hope is practical. It is not wishful thinking. Hope is applied faith (Hebrews 11:1). It is confidence that the future can be better than the past. Hope allows you to live by inspiration rather than resignation. Hope awakens your spiritual capacities. It makes you more thoughtful and purposeful. It gives you direction and energy. It produces health and wellness.

Hope is tactical. Success is a result of sustained thought and continuous effort. When you hope for something, you think about it a lot. Hope allows you to see your longings as if they were accomplished. Your vision becomes clearer, and your motivation becomes stronger. Hope transforms a desire into a goal and a goal into reality. It excites the imagination, ignites passion, and sparks action. Hope is to the soul what wood is to a fire or gasoline is to an engine. It is the fuel of spiritual growth and positive change.

When you hope for something, you also talk about it a lot: in prayer to God, in discussions with others, and in conversations with yourself. When you visualize and verbalize the solution to a problem, you have a start. When you strategize and mobilize, you have success. There is no room for pessimism when you are busy praying, planning, and preparing for good things to happen (Nehemiah 6:1-9).

Hope is invincible. It summons the best of everything God placed within you. It challenges you to make the best of situations and of yourself. Hope is not denial or delusion. Rather, it is walking by faith. Hope enables you to reframe events and adjust your attitude in accord with God's promises. Hope is the anchor of the soul that keeps you from being swept away by doubt and discouragement. The tide of negative emotions that drowns most people's dreams cannot overwhelm a believer buoyed by faith and stabilized by hope. No momentary problem can defeat you, not even the worst life has to offer (2 Corinthians 4:8, 16). You know in due season that you will reap if you do not give up (Galatians 6:9). This is the power of hope.

Positive People Are People of Love

Love is proven. If you ask someone to do something that puts her character, reputation, health, or future at risk, your motive is not love. Love is caring action and responsible choice. Love of this kind can accomplish what no other power on earth can. Paul said it is more powerful than money or miracles (1 Corinthians 13:1-4). Love is the power of God at work in your will. You show your love for God by loving the people He puts around you. Good intentions are nice, but actions are what counts (Matthew 6:21). Love is as love does. Consider the following examples.

Love is preventive. It does no harm to others (Romans 13:10). Paul made a list of things love does not do (1 Corinthians 13:4). Love does not envy or boast. It is not arrogant or rude. Love does not insist on its own way. It is not irritable or resentful. Love does not rejoice at wrongdoing. These are traits of an unloving person despite claims to the contrary. Love places a protective boundary around the people in your life.

Love is productive. Paul also provided a list of love's positive features (1 Corinthians 13:4). Love is patient and kind (Galatians 5:22). It rejoices with the truth and speaks the truth in love (Ephesians 4:15). Because love believes and hopes all things, it can bear and endure all things. Loving people bear the worst, believe the best, hope the most, and endure the rest. This is the power of love.

The point is that loving people live responsible lives. They do not injure or burden others needlessly. They carry their own loads and bear others' burdens. Unloving people live irresponsible lives. They harm or neglect others. They burden rather than bless. When you strip away the unloving parts of your life, Christ comes increasingly into view (Galatians 2:20). Love is the irreducible essence of a Christlike life (Ephesians 4:15-16).

SOLVING PROBLEMS REQUIRES CHANGE

Change begins with repentance (*metanoia*). More than remorse, repentance requires a complete change of heart that transforms your attitude and behavior (Matthew 22:37). Jesus said, "Repent, for the kingdom of heaven is at hand" (4:17). Eternity is coming, but heaven draws closer anytime you become more Christlike. If you are satisfied with the old you, it will keep you from becoming the best you (16:25). Repentance is a repudiation of the past to embrace a better future.

The real obstacle to happiness is not your neighbor or your circumstances. Unhappiness stems from unholy attitudes and selfish behaviors. It is habitually choosing ineffective ways of dealing with problems and stress. It is choosing doubt, fear, and selfishness over faith, hope, and love. It is judging and criticizing people who disappoint you. Sadness and loneliness come from inventing slights, assuming motives, and exaggerating problems. When you turn down the heat and turn up the respect, mountain-size problems return to molehill proportions.

Caring, constructive actions solve most problems over time. Regardless, it is the only sensible way to live (Romans 12:17-18). Love for God produces love for those made in His image. Love for Christ produces love in those made in His image.

SOLVING PROBLEMS REQUIRES CHOICE

Problems are real, but so is God's love. Though some problems will not be solved in this lifetime, God will comfort your heart until the day He wipes away the last tear from your eyes. You may be grieved now for a little while, but peace is possible even in the midst of hardship. It all depends on where you focus your attention and affection.

If your heart is hurting today, look to Jesus with eyes full of faith and a heart full of hope (Hebrews 12:1-2). Look beyond what frustrates you to your Father. Look beyond your pain to His power. Look beyond your misery to His mercy. And look beyond the moment to eternity. Look beyond earthly loss to heavenly gain. Look beyond the grave to glory. Look beyond the burden you bear to the cross He carried.

There is a sequence in Paul's list. First comes faith, hope follows, and love is the end. Every good thing begins with faith. Faith enables you to see with insight rather than eyesight (2 Corinthians 5:7). Do you see Him at the cross dying for your sins? Do you see Him raised, glorified, and ready to be revealed again? Do you see Him seated at God's right hand, interceding for you? Do you see Him with angels shouting and trumpets blasting as He returns to rescue you from all the problems and pain ever experienced in this world? Do you see Him at heaven's gate, smiling as He welcomes you into the joy of your Lord?

Problems are inevitable, but unhappiness is a choice. The key to living positively, constructively, and eternally is the power of the gospel. If you want to live by God's infinite power rather than your limited power, begin by embracing those things that abide. Through faith in Christ, hope in the future, and love without end, you can triumph over life's troubles. In the process, you will also become a more considerate person.

Positivity

SELF-ASSESSMENT

Y N 1. Do I think hopeful thoughts?

Y N 2. Do I think caring thoughts?

Y N 3. Do I think joyful thoughts?

Y N 4. Do I think thankful thoughts?

Y N 5. Do I think realistic, constructive thoughts?

QUESTIONS

1. Man who is born of woman is few of what (Job 14:1)?

2. Man who is born of woman is full of what (Job 14:1)?

3. What are three indispensable things that abide
   (1 Corinthians 13:13)?

4. When you strip away unlovely parts of your life, who comes
   into view (Galatians 2:20)?

5. What turns troubled people into trusting people (John 14:1)?

DISCUSSION

1. How are problems like waves slapping on the seashore?

2. How do unrealistic expectations rob you of joy?

3. Why are negative expectations prophetic?

4. How does faith make your life better?

5. How does hope make your life better?

6. How does love make your life better?

7. Why are unholy attitudes the real obstacles to happiness?

8. Why is unhappiness a choice?

EXERCISE

List three ways your congregation (or family) will become more positive.

1

2

3

CHAPTER 12
Be Forgiving

When you forgive, you in no way change the past—
but you sure do change the future.

—Bernard Meltzer

Will God forgive sins you do not specifically repent of by name? I sure hope so, for there are some sins during your lifetime of which you will never be aware. I do not know that grace will cover presumptuous sins, but it does make provision for some inadvertent ones. Sin does not have to be purposeful to be harmful to you or others, but perfect understanding and flawless performance are not God's expectation. Imperfect repentance is among the many things the Almighty can forgive.

All noncompliance is not the same. Disobedience can be due to defiance, carelessness, or ignorance (sometimes willful, sometimes not). Mitigating factors are taken into account by judges both human and divine. Since God can read hearts, His judgments are perfect (Jeremiah 17:10). Lacking that capacity, it is advisable to give others the benefit of the doubt when judgment rests with you. Realize that, in the course of your life (especially your married life), a portion of the fault in disagreements must be yours even though you sincerely believe you are correct. In human affairs, there will be honest disagreements to navigate if you are to keep the unity of the Spirit in the bond of peace (Ephesians 4:1-3).

Repenting of specific sins speeds healing, learning, and growth. It is to be expected in cases where moral lapses are obvious. Yet the fault in some cases is not always clear. Harm may have occurred that was unintentional. The offending act may have arisen from misguided compassion (though the assessment of the motive may be biased). Of the many things our merciful God will forgive, might occasional lack of self-awareness be one? And what does that say about our forgiveness of others?

OVERCOMING THE PAST

How do people get over a hurtful past? How could South Africa find healing after generations of apartheid? Nelson Mandela chose a policy of racial reconciliation as he battled institutional racism. It would take both grace and good government to move forward.

How did Abraham Lincoln seek to reunify Northerners and Southerners after bitter disputes and bloody battles in America? In his second inaugural address, on March 4, 1865, he closed with these generous words:

> With malice toward none, with charity for all, with firmness in the right as God gives us to see the right, let us strive on to finish the work we are in, to bind up the nation's wounds, to care for him who shall have borne the battle and for his widow and his orphan, to do all which may achieve and cherish a just and lasting peace among ourselves and with all nations.

These were wise and timely words. Some had sincerely defended their state while others conscientiously defended their country. Lincoln focused their minds away from the painful past to a hopeful, peaceful future they could build together.

In our modern world of self-righteous social activism that
demonizes opponents and justifies any means to achieve its ends,
we see the fruits of intolerance in the name of righteousness
(James 3:14-16). Let us be careful not to repeat this error in the
church (Galatians 5:15). Forgiveness is the only sensible path
to a future worth living. Patterns of evil must be opposed, but
forbearance comes highly recommended as a way of handling
interpersonal conflict (Ephesians 4:2). Without forgiveness
and forbearance, meaningful relationships are not possible in
churches, families, or any other social setting. These are essential
skills to be cultivated and practiced by the truly righteous.

So, are you more interested in helping others get right or
proving you are right? Kindness and patience can bring people
around in ways judging and condemning never will. Give people
time and understanding instead of prosecuting every wrong.
The hypersensitive and overscrupulous can do more to damage
a church than perceived offenders. Tolerating chronic fault-
finding results in a toxic atmosphere that inhibits growth in the
church. Healthy people avoid it. Unhealthy people imitate it. The
compounding effects of a culture of criticism are foreseeable,
regrettable, and preventable. Do not reward it. Redirect it.

THE SIMPLICITY OF FORGIVENESS

God's call to forgive is clear and direct. It reminds me of the
simplicity of God's command to honor parents. Sadly, some Jews
came up with a way to ignore God's will while pretending to
honor Him. Just declare your wealth "Corban," devoted to God,
and hold on to your money for your lifetime (Mark 7:11). God
was not amused by their plan.

Something similar happens when people set aside straightfor-
ward commands to forgive while framing nonaction as virtuous.
The tenor of the New Testament's teaching on forgiveness is

plain: forgive freely and eagerly. In fact, Scripture clearly states there will be no forgiveness from God for those who do not forgive their fellow man. Sobering words indeed.

Then, someone comes along and says you cannot forgive unrepentant people. Suddenly, forgiveness becomes complicated. You are supposedly under divine obligation to withhold what God repeatedly said to give. This view is based on an erroneous inference drawn from a fine point of grammar in a single passage: "Pay attention to yourselves! If your brother sins, rebuke him, and if he repents, forgive him" (Luke 17:3 ESV). Is the verse saying you should forgive "only if" or "certainly if"? Is the gist "do not forgive unless and until one repents," or does it mean "in the likelihood that a person asks for your forgiveness, by all means, give it"? Grammatically speaking, repentance is a felicitous occasion for forgiveness, not a precondition.

Yet, to make the position tenable, advocates claim they are merely imitating God since He makes "repentance" requisite for the forgiveness of sins (Ephesians 5:1). This reasoning allows you to hold on to your grudge while positioning yourself as righteous, but it also raises a question. If, in addition to repentance, God requires faith and baptism to forgive sin, can I only forgive someone who is a baptized believer (4:32)? Clearly, interpersonal forgiveness on earth is not the same as judicial forgiveness in the court of heaven.

Merely expressing a *willingness* to forgive when the offending party confesses fault is not imitating God. It is putting yourself in the place of God (a very lofty place from which to fall). You are not worthy or capable of such a post. Better to let offenses go and trust God to make things right. And do not forget you will be judged based on your forgiveness of others—not your willingness to forgive (when they come to their senses) but whether you actually forgave. Did you, or didn't you?

So, let us take a closer look at these positions and consider the real-world outcomes. The first is conditional forgiveness, meaning you must repent before I forgive you. The second is unconditional forgiveness, meaning I can choose to forgive you without preconditions.

CONDITIONAL FORGIVENESS

1. *Keeps a record of wrongs.*
   Love "keeps no record of wrongs" (1 Corinthians 13:5 NIV) and "is not ... resentful" (ESV).

2. *Puts me in bondage to you until you realize you are wrong.*
   For freedom Christ has set us free; stand firm therefore, and do not submit again to a yoke of slavery. (Galatians 5:1 ESV)

3. *Necessitates judging.*
   Judge not, that you be not judged. For with the judgment you pronounce you will be judged, and with the measure you use it will be measured to you. (Matthew 7:1-2 ESV)

4. *Creates an impasse in marriage.*
   And whenever you stand praying, forgive, if you have anything against anyone, so that your Father also who is in heaven may forgive you your trespasses. (Mark 11:25 ESV)

5. *Produces a toxic atmosphere in churches.*
   I entreat Euodia and I entreat Syntyche to agree in the Lord. Yes, I ask you also, true companion, help these women, who have labored side by side with me in the gospel together with Clement and the rest of my fellow

workers, whose names are in the book of life. (Philippians 4:2-3 ESV)

But if you bite and devour one another, watch out that you are not consumed by one another. (Galatians 5:15 ESV)

6. *Negates plain teaching on forgiveness.*
   For if you forgive others their trespasses, your heavenly Father will also forgive you, but if you do not forgive others their trespasses, neither will your Father forgive your trespasses. (Matthew 6:14-15 ESV)

7. *Elevates me to the place of God.*
   But Joseph said to them, "Do not fear, for am I in the place of God?" (Genesis 50:19 ESV)

8. *Singles out repentance but neglects faith and baptism to forgive like God.*
   And Peter said to them, "Repent and be baptized every one of you in the name of Jesus Christ for the forgiveness of your sins, and you will receive the gift of the Holy Spirit." (Acts 2:38 ESV)

9. *Is burdensome and polarizing (it leaves people weary, conflicted, and stuck).*
   Come to me, all who labor and are heavy laden, and I will give you rest. Take my yoke upon you, and learn from me, for I am gentle and lowly in heart, and you will find rest for your souls. (Matthew 11:28-29 ESV)

10. *Is undoable.*

Now, therefore, why are you putting God to the test by placing a yoke on the neck of the disciples that neither our fathers nor we have been able to bear? (Acts 15:10 ESV)

UNCONDITIONAL FORGIVENESS

1. *Is personal forgiveness, not divine forgiveness.*
   Who can forgive sins but God alone? (Mark 2:7 ESV)

2. *Does not affect your salvation but does affect mine.*
   For judgment is without mercy to one who has shown no mercy. Mercy triumphs over judgment. (James 2:13 ESV)

3. *Is more about me and God than you and me.*
   Be merciful, even as your Father is merciful.
   (Luke 6:36 ESV)

4. *Recognizes my human limitations (I am not all-knowing or capable of pure love).*
   And no creature is hidden from his sight, but all are naked and exposed to the eyes of him to whom we must give account. (Hebrews 4:13 ESV)

5. *Leaves no outstanding debt (unfinished business) but love.*
   Owe no one anything, except to love each other, for the one who loves another has fulfilled the law.
   (Romans 13:8 ESV)

6. *Obeys God without exception or explanation.*
   Put on then, as God's chosen ones, holy and beloved, compassionate hearts, kindness, humility, meekness, and patience, bearing with one another and, if one has

a complaint against another, forgiving each other; as the Lord has forgiven you, so you also must forgive. (Colossians 3:12-13 ESV)

7. *Admits there are ways I am incapable of imitating God.*
Beloved, never avenge yourselves, but leave it to the wrath of God, for it is written, "Vengeance is mine, I will repay, says the Lord." (Romans 12:19 ESV)

8. *Follows notable examples of what to do when people don't realize wrongs.*
And Jesus said, "Father, forgive them, for they know not what they do." (Luke 23:34 ESV)

And falling to his knees he cried out with a loud voice, "Lord, do not hold this sin against them." And when he had said this, he fell asleep. (Acts 7:60 ESV)

9. *Is simple, liberating, and gracious (leaves me free, at peace, able to move on).*
Good sense makes one slow to anger, and it is his glory to overlook an offense. (Proverbs 19:11 ESV)

10. *Obeys God rather than men. (God says do forgive, don't judge. Men say don't forgive, do judge.)*
But Peter and the apostles answered, "We must obey God rather than men." (Acts 5:29 ESV)

Conditional forgiveness requires some special accessories. You will need a notebook to record people's wrongs, a judge's gavel to pronounce their faults, and a royal scepter to convey your eminence. Unconditional forgiveness has but one requirement: a willing heart.

There is no promise of God's forgiveness without repentance, but that does not mean I cannot forgive someone who does not repent. Our natures, powers, and roles are different from God's in significant ways. Conditional forgiveness is unworkable for mortals due to the human condition. Unconditional forgiveness is better suited to our needs and nature.

Falling in love with God makes you eager to forgive the fallen. Why? Because those who are forgiven much, love much in return (Luke 7:47). Imitating His grace makes your relationships richer, and emulating His mercy makes your life abundant. Choose forgiveness.

Forgiveness

SELF-ASSESSMENT

Y N 1. Do I keep a record of wrongs?

Y N 2. Do I judge people's motives?

Y N 3. Do I leave redress to God?

Y N 4. Do I forgive like Jesus and Stephen when people hurt me?

Y N 5. Do I forgive as I was forgiven and as I hope to be forgiven?

QUESTIONS

1. What must Christians endeavor to keep (Ephesians 4:3)?

2. What does Paul recommend for handling interpersonal conflict (Ephesians 4:2)?

3. What word did Jews use to sidestep a command of God (Mark 7:11)?

4. Circumcision is a matter of the heart by the what (Romans 2:29)?

5. What must churches avoid (Galatians 5:15)?

DISCUSSION

1. What is the difference between personal and divine forgiveness?

2. Is forgiveness more about you and me or me and God?

3. How do human limitations bear on human forgiveness?

4. What did Jesus recommend when people do not realize they are wrong?

5. What do you appreciate about the simplicity of biblical forgiveness?

6. How is biblical forgiveness liberating?

7. How might conditional forgiveness create an impasse in marriage?

8. How might conditional forgiveness create a toxic atmosphere in churches?

EXERCISE

List three ways your congregation (or
family) will become more forgiving.

1

2

3

CHAPTER 13
Be Christlike

Could a greater miracle take place than for us to
look through each other's eyes for an instant?

—Henry David Thoreau

This book began with a plea for civility from the pen of Paul. He wrote, "Do nothing from selfish ambition or conceit, but in humility count others more significant than yourselves. Let each of you look not only to his own interests, but also to the interests of others" (Philippians 2:3-4 ESV). These words are especially noteworthy against the backdrop of Paul's early life. Before meeting Christ, humility and empathy were not Paul's leading qualities. He was religious and zealous, but he was not kind or considerate.

A Christian life is a considerate life. In the context of human history, inconsiderateness seems like a small sin, almost unworthy of notice. The word "inconsiderate" means to cause hurt thoughtlessly. Indeed, most of the world's pain is caused by carelessness. As you eliminate little acts of insensitivity from your life, larger ones usually take care of themselves. But ignore the little ones, and as James said, "Sin when it is fully grown brings forth death" (James 1:15 ESV).

Seemingly small sins have huge consequences. Inconsiderateness can lead to the death of treasured relationships. It also can lead to the death of your soul. Darkened minds, seared consciences, and hardened hearts occur when human faculties lose their sensitivity to God's will and people's needs. However small they be, beware of inconsiderate remarks and thoughtless deeds.

THE MAN (Acts 8:1-3)

Saul the Pharisee was selfish, ambitious, and perhaps a little conceited. He climbed the ladder of success on the backs of people he destroyed. You cannot do what Saul did and be sensitive to other people's feelings. You must go stone-cold to be that mean.

Luke said Paul ravaged the church. To ravage something is to ruin or devastate it. The people Saul persecuted were not a danger to others. They were not even disturbing the peace. Nonetheless, he hunted them down and entered their homes without invitation. He would drag women out of their houses, away from the arms of loved ones, and confine them in primitive prisons. In stark contrast to this brutality, he carefully protected the coats of his colleagues to keep them clean, safe, and unwrinkled while they took stones to break men's bones and crush the life from their bodies.

When Saul was not persecuting Christians, he was thinking and talking about it. He boasted he would do more and worse things. He vented, ranted, and threatened. Without the slightest embarrassment or hesitation, he publicly expressed his intent to slaughter his countrymen with whom he had religious differences. He spoke of violently and cruelly killing followers of Christ. When you do not know people personally, it is far easier to mistreat them. Saul felt justified in his vile actions because he judged all Christians deserving of death. Then, one day, everything changed.

THE MEETING (Acts 9:1-9)

Saul was en route to Damascus to arrest Christians and return them to Jerusalem to stand trial and face punishment. He possessed letters from the high priest giving him legal authority to apprehend these criminals fleeing justice, but the day would not end as he expected. Jesus, who appeared on earth in the fullness of time to save sinners (Galatians 4:4), made a special appearance to save the worst of all sinners (1 Timothy 1:15). Saul was the true lawbreaker skirting divine justice, and Jesus was coming to make an arrest.

As they approached the outskirts of the city, a burst of light robbed Saul of his eyesight. The flash drove him from his mount to the ground. From this humble position, the proud persecutor heard a voice from heaven: "Saul, Saul, why are you persecuting Me?" (Acts 9:4). Jesus revealed His identity and directed Saul to enter the city, where he would be told what to do.

Saul's companions led him by the hand to a residence on Straight Street in Damascus. They must have pitied the helpless man before them. The once intimidating figure was now weak and powerless. It seemed like the worst thing that could have happened to Saul. In fact, it was the best. It was exactly what he needed to awaken him from spiritual blindness brought on by pure hatred. Now, his eyes would be opened to the power and possibilities of love.

THE MESSENGER (Acts 9:10-19a)

After three days of soul-searching, Saul received a message from Jesus. The news came from a reluctant messenger named Ananias. Saul entered people's houses to harm them, but Ananias came to help him. Ananias was hesitant to approach Saul due to his ferocious reputation, but the Lord assured him things were different now. Saul's heart was captive to Christ, and he would work even harder to advance the gospel than he had previously to oppose it.

Ananias came to heal Saul's eyes, save his soul, and prepare him for service. First, he laid hands on him to restore his sight. Next, he baptized him for forgiveness. Finally, he told Saul that God had selected him to be His missionary to the Gentiles. In an amazing turn of events, this once angry, insensitive man was now on a mission to rescue the world from all the inhumane effects of sin with which he was personally acquainted. The world looked very different now that he saw it through Jesus' eyes. Awakened, forgiven, and commissioned, he was eager to do for others what had been done for him. This was conversion at its best.

THE MINISTER (Acts 9:19b-22)

A convincing evidence of Jesus' resurrection is the astounding change in the life of Saul. Explaining his transformation, he declared, "I have been crucified with Christ. It is no longer I who live, but Christ who lives in me. And the life I now live in the flesh I live by faith in the Son of God, who loved me and gave himself for me" (Galatians 2:20 ESV). What does it mean to live by faith in the Son of God? It means to trust Him implicitly.

Saul's experience on the road to Damascus convinced him Jesus was Lord, but he also believed Jesus loved him. Knowing he was undeserving of such mercy, he began and ended every letter celebrating God's grace and the peace it afforded. Through grace, Saul was forgiven of all the hateful, hurtful things he had ever done to other people. When Saul realized how much Jesus loved him, he also experienced a peace that passes all understanding. A peaceful life is marked by wellness and wholeness. Loving people are kind and calm. Unloving people are turbulent and troublesome. Damaged relationships evidence souls lacking grace and peace.

THE MODEL (Philippians 2:5)

Paul became a channel of the grace and peace he received from God. He preached it and practiced it. Consequently, one of the world's most inconsiderate men became a model of Christlikeness. Paul used his example to challenge and inspire others. He told the Corinthians, "Be imitators of me, as I am of Christ" (1 Corinthians 11:1 ESV). Imitators mimic the speech and actions of another. Some do it to mock or entertain. In this case, the goal is to edify and glorify.

Paul often called on people to follow him, but the goal was never self-promotion (1 Corinthians 4:16; Philippians 3:17; 2 Thessalonians 3:7, 9). He used his example to help people know and follow Christ. Every day, he would show people the beauty and benefits of Christian living (Philippians 1:21). By following someone who is faithfully following Christ, you become more Christlike. The best part is that following Christ produces joy in your life and in the lives of those around you (1 Thessalonians 1:6).

Misery-producing people have a choice. They can awaken to the devastation they inflict on those around them, or they can die lonely, despised, self-righteous, and unprepared for judgment. Jesus confronted Saul on the road to Damascus, and He is confronting you here and now on the road to your future. Jesus' teaching and example are bursts of heavenly light that allow you to see the awfulness of insensitivity and the attractiveness of considerateness. Ananias was sent to open Saul's eyes, and this book was written to open your eyes. Can you see the faces of people you have been injuring or ignoring? Do you see the opportunities for thoughtfulness and kindness you have been overlooking?

The goal of life is Christlikeness, and the essence of Christlikeness is considerateness. Love is the greatest command, yet what is love but kindness that stems from thoughtfulness?

I cannot love you without first thinking of you. That is why consideration is the foundation of love and the basis of all the good you will do in your lifetime. It makes you careful not to hurt, inconvenience, or burden others needlessly. However, desiring not to harm others is insufficient. You must endeavor to help and bless them.

Love is proactive as well as protective. That is why the Golden Rule is the supreme law of life. Think of the Golden Rule as a spiritual app: a mobile version of the great commandment stored conveniently in your memory. You can take it with you everywhere and apply it in any situation. It is doing others good by considering their needs as you reflect on your own desires. It takes the warm impulses of your heart and turns them into instant action. Empathy is the indispensable quality of a considerate life.

THE MINDSET

David marveled at the attentiveness of God in caring for mankind. He wrote, "What is man that you are mindful of him, and the son of man that you care for him?" (Psalm 8:4 ESV). Mindfulness is the essence of love, and Jesus modeled this mindset for His disciples. To possess the mind of Christ is to be constantly aware of and consistently attentive to the needs of others.

In the beginning, Jesus was thinking of you when He created the world with all its delights. All colors, smells, textures, sounds, and tastes were made with humanity in mind (although some smells make you wonder). Jesus was thinking of you when the world was plunged into sin by the careless actions of Adam and Eve. Paradise was lost, death became reality, and pain entered everyday life. Obviously, their plan was not well considered, but God's response was. In due time, the seed of woman (Christ) would crush the head of Satan (Genesis 3:15). In Eden, Jesus was already thinking of you.

Sin increased on the earth until God sent a flood to stop the spread of wickedness. During the deluge, Jesus was thinking of you. He knew the flood foreshadowed the spiritual reset that would occur one day at baptism. Peter wrote, "Baptism, which corresponds to this, now saves you, not as a removal of dirt from the body but as an appeal to God for a good conscience, through the resurrection of Jesus Christ" (1 Peter 3:21 ESV).

Later, the call of Abraham set in motion God's plan for saving mankind. As the scheme of redemption unfolded, Jesus was thinking of you each step of the way. He once told a group of argumentative Jews, "Before Abraham was, I AM" (John 8:58). Paul noted the remarkable link between the father of the faithful, his true children, and Jesus. He wrote, "And if you are Christ's, then you are Abraham's offspring, heirs according to promise" (Galatians 3:29 ESV). Throughout sacred history, Christ was working on your behalf.

Jesus was thinking of you when He arrived from heaven on the greatest rescue mission of all time. Leaving the beauty and safety of heaven was a monumental expression of love. To be born in a manger in an obscure village was a message and not an accident. It said, "I love you more than anything in the world." It asks, "What do you love first and most?"

During three years of ministry, Jesus thought of you. He had three short years to prepare a team to fulfill His dream for you. He was not preoccupied by amusements or diversions. He was not obsessed with acquiring and consuming this world's goods. His life was not about money, pleasure, or fame. One thing was on His mind when He got up, and one thing was on His mind when He went to sleep. All kindnesses, conversations, parables, sermons, and miracles were acts of determined love for you.

In Gethsemane, Jesus was thinking of you when He entered the garden to pray. He knew He would not leave a free man. He was sorrowful unto death, yet unafraid to die. At Golgotha, Christ was thinking of you as He hung on the cross. Inside the tomb, He was thinking of you on the day He arose.

Jesus was thinking of you when He left earth to return to glory. In heaven, He presented His blood to atone for your sins. From heaven, He sent His Spirit to comfort, guide, and pray for you. From God's right hand, He intercedes for you. Every Lord's Day, He communes with you. At this moment, He is preparing a place for you. He is ever eager to return to you. In the meantime, He promised never to leave or forsake you. Imagine the depth of love that produces such thoughtfulness. It boggles the mind and thrills the heart.

THE MOTIVATION

Jesus said whoever will save his life will lose it, but whoever will lose his life will save it. If anyone understood the meaning of these words, it was Saul of Tarsus. Saul went from worst to first: worst enemy of Christ to leading apostle to the Gentiles. He went from hater and persecutor of Christians to lover and imitator of Christ. Saul's faith *in* Christ and love *for* Christ were the difference makers in his life. They can do the same for you.

According to Jesus, judgment will include a realistic assessment of how considerate you were during your days on earth (Matthew 25:31-36). The writer of Hebrews concurred,

> And *let us consider* how to stir up one another to love and good works, not neglecting to meet together, as is the habit of some, but encouraging one another, and all the more as you see the Day drawing near. (10:24-25 ESV)

In the preceding verses, the writer listed two preconditions for becoming a considerate person. You must draw near and hold fast.

> Therefore, brothers, since we have confidence to enter the holy places by the blood of Jesus, by the new and living way that he opened for us through the curtain, that is, through his flesh, and since we have a great priest over the house of God, *let us draw near* with a true heart in full assurance of faith, with our hearts sprinkled clean from an evil conscience and our bodies washed with pure water. *Let us hold fast* the confession of our hope without wavering, for he who promised is faithful. (vv. 19-23 ESV)

Those who "draw near" to Jesus appreciate His love. Those who "hold fast" to Jesus imitate His love. The goal is not only to be *with* Christ but to be *like* Christ. The result of this nearness and resoluteness is improved relationships.

In the beginning, empathy is difficult to develop. In the end, it is instinctive though imperfect. At the start, it is awkward and erratic. Over time, it becomes graceful and joyful. Through patient practice, empathy is a mindset that becomes a skill set.

Christianity is a practical and positive religion. It is about your daily life as well as eternal life. So, let us consider how to stir up love and good works. Let us be tireless, creative, and bold in the practice of mindfulness. Thank You, Lord, for revealing to us the answer to incivility (Colossians 1:27). Help us, Lord, to be more like Your blessed Son.

Christlikeness

SELF-ASSESSMENT

Y N 1. Do I think of others more than myself?

Y N 2. Do I think of God's will more than my will?

Y N 3. Do I think of ways to stir up love and good works?

Y N 4. Do I deny myself and bear others' burdens?

Y N 5. Do I live by the Golden Rule?

QUESTIONS

1. What enables you to count others more significant (Philippians 2:4)?

2. What do small sins give birth to when fully grown (James 1:15)?

3. Whom did Paul imitate to become a new man (1 Corinthians 11:1)?

4. Name two preconditions for becoming considerate (Hebrews 10:19-25).

5. What is the ultimate answer to incivility (Colossians 1:27)?

DISCUSSION

1. What was Paul like before and after his conversion?

2. How do you account for the difference?

3. Are most sins against others intentional or careless?

4. What are some ways people thoughtlessly hurt others?

5. Why are loving people kinder and calmer?

6. Why are unloving people turbulent and troublesome?

7. How do you practice mindfulness?

8. How might you do even better?

EXERCISE

List three ways your congregation (or family) will become more Christlike.

1

2

3

Afterword

You cannot do a kindness too soon, for you
never know how soon it will be too late.

—Ralph Waldo Emerson

If we lift up Christ and fix our eyes on Him, something new and wonderful can happen in our times. Like at Pentecost, the blood of Christ and the gospel of peace can bring dying people closer together "to the praise of his glorious grace" (Ephesians 1:6a ESV).

In times of stress, people are prone to lash out at their neighbors, mates, or brethren rather than probe their own hearts. In times of tension, may we search our hearts for a way forward that will please God, honor His Word, and bless our fellow man (Philippians 2:1-2). When feeling pressured, may we elevate our Lord rather than our differences. Christ said, "And I, when I am lifted up from the earth, will draw all people to myself" (John 12:32 ESV). He did not promise to resolve all human differences, but He guaranteed that hearts focused on Him will grow closer as a result.

In closing, let us recall Paul's beautiful declaration of the spiritual benefits belonging to those in Christ. These words describe not only blessings to be enjoyed but also a charge to be fulfilled.

> In him we have redemption through his blood, the forgiveness of our trespasses, according to the riches of his grace, which he lavished upon us, in all wisdom and insight making

known to us the mystery of his will, according to his purpose, which he set forth in Christ as a plan for the fullness of
time, to unite all things in him, things in heaven and things
on earth. (Ephesians 1:7-10 ESV)

To promote civility and prepare for eternity, may we lift up our
Lord, proclaim redemption through His blood, declare the riches
of His grace, and unite all things in Him—to the praise of His
glorious grace.

Be Mindful

God's answer to incivility is to consider one another. Awareness of others—their presence, feelings, and needs—is fundamental to civility in society and to Christlikeness in your soul. Before you can love others, you must notice them. Sin comes from overlooking others—their presence or pain. Those who ignore or abuse people displease God, who made them in His image. Consequently, the Lord filled the Bible with admonitions to be mindful of others. It is striking how many "one another" passages there are in God's Word.

Citizens of heaven possess a mindset that distinguishes them as God's children (Philippians 2:5). As you meditate on the following passages and faithfully practice them, you will increasingly resemble the Lord.[3] Thus, heaven's antidote to rudeness is simple: follow Jesus. The more you walk in His footsteps, the more thoughtful you are. The more thoughtful you are, the kinder you become. The kinder you become, the more heaven comes to earth. May mercy, peace, and love be multiplied to you and through you (Jude 2).

Bearing with One Another

... with all humility and gentleness, with patience, bearing with one another in love. (Ephesians 4:2)

... bearing with one another and, if one has a complaint against another, forgiving each other; as the Lord has forgiven you, so you also must forgive. (Colossians 3:13)

Encourage One Another

Therefore encourage one another and build one another up, just as you are doing. (1 Thessalonians 5:11)

... not neglecting to meet together, as is the habit of some, but encouraging one another, and all the more as you see the Day drawing near. (Hebrews 10:25)

Greet One Another

Greet one another with a holy kiss. All the churches of Christ greet you. (Romans 16:16)

All the brothers send you greetings. Greet one another with a holy kiss. (1 Corinthians 16:20)

Greet one another with a holy kiss. (2 Corinthians 13:12)

Greet one another with the kiss of love. Peace to all of you who are in Christ. (1 Peter 5:14)

Love One Another

A new commandment I give to you, that you love one another: just as I have loved you, you also are to love one another. (John 13:34)

By this all people will know that you are my disciples, if you have love for one another. (John 13:35)

Love one another with brotherly affection. Outdo one another in showing honor. (Romans 12:10)

Having purified your souls by your obedience to the truth for a sincere brotherly love, love one another earnestly from a pure heart. (1 Peter 1:22)

For this is the message that you have heard from the beginning, that we should love one another. (1 John 3:11)

And this is his commandment, that we believe in the name of his Son Jesus Christ and love one another, just as he has commanded us. (1 John 3:23)

Beloved, let us love one another, for love is from God, and whoever loves has been born of God and knows God. (1 John 4:7)

Beloved, if God so loved us, we also ought to love one another. (1 John 4:11)

No one has ever seen God; if we love one another, God abides in us and his love is perfected in us. (1 John 4:12)

And now I ask you, dear lady—not as though I were writing you a new commandment, but the one we have had from the beginning—that we love one another. (2 John 1:5)

Negative One Another Passages

Do not speak evil against one another, brothers. The one who speaks against a brother or judges his brother, speaks evil against the law and judges the law. But if you judge the law, you are not a doer of the law but a judge. (James 4:11)

Therefore let us not pass judgment on one another any longer, but rather decide never to put a stumbling block or hindrance in the way of a brother. (Romans 14:13)

Miscellaneous One Another Passages

If I then, your Lord and Teacher, have washed your feet, you also ought to wash one another's feet. (John 13:14)

Live in harmony with one another. Do not be haughty, but associate with the lowly. Never be wise in your own sight. (Romans 12:16)

Therefore welcome one another as Christ has welcomed you, for the glory of God. (Romans 15:7)

For you were called to freedom, brothers. Only do not use your freedom as an opportunity for the flesh, but through love serve one another. (Galatians 5:13)

Be kind to one another, tenderhearted, forgiving one another, as God in Christ forgave you. (Ephesians 4:32)

... addressing one another in psalms and hymns and spiritual songs, singing and making melody to the Lord with your heart. (Ephesians 5:19)

... submitting to one another out of reverence for Christ. (Ephesians 5:21)

Let the word of Christ dwell in you richly, teaching and admonishing one another in all wisdom, singing psalms and hymns and spiritual songs, with thankfulness in your hearts to God. (Colossians 3:16)

But exhort one another every day, as long as it is called "today," that none of you may be hardened by the deceitfulness of sin. (Hebrews 3:13)

And let us consider how to stir up one another to love and good works. (Hebrews 10:24)

Show hospitality to one another without grumbling. (1 Peter 4:9)

Likewise, you who are younger, be subject to the elders. Clothe yourselves, all of you, with humility toward one another, for "God opposes the proud but gives grace to the humble." (1 Peter 5:5)

But if we walk in the light, as he is in the light, we have fellowship with one another, and the blood of Jesus his Son cleanses us from all sin. (1 John 1:7)

Answers to Questions

Chapter 1—Be Considerate

1. The Golden Rule
2. Empathy
3. Pray for them, bless them, do good to them
4. Civility, productivity, happiness, unity
5. A tender heart

Chapter 2—Be Kind

1. Because He first loved us
2. A cheerful heart
3. Sin and selfishness (whatever holds me back from becoming my best)
4. The weak and ungodly
5. Whatever he or she sows

Chapter 3—Be Friendly

1. To sense the needs of those around you
2. Loving actions (not just words)
3. Greet one another
4. A simple, sincere greeting
5. By bearing one another's burdens

Chapter 4—Be Compassionate

1. Deuteronomy 6:5 and Leviticus 19:18
2. A priest and a Levite
3. A Samaritan
4. The one who showed mercy
5. Go and do likewise

Chapter 5—Be Present

1. Sin
2. Expressing his own opinion
3. Unspoken words
4. Bridle them
5. God

Chapter 6—Be Courteous

1. Exalt yourself
2. Eye-service and people-pleasing
3. He will be humbled
4. Highly exalted Him
5. Heavenly places

Chapter 7—Be Merciful

1. Justice, mercy, and humility
2. The Father of mercies and God of all comfort
3. They shall obtain mercy
4. That God might show all longsuffering
5. Mercy, peace, and love multiplied

Chapter 8—Be Hospitable

1. The table of showbread
2. A table
3. The Shunammite woman
4. 150 Jews and rulers
5. The queen of Sheba

Chapter 9—Be Understanding

1. God is forgiving, good, and abounding in love
2. So we can run
3. Cast them upon the Lord

4. The steadfast love of the Lord

5. Ahab

Chapter 10—Be Responsible

1. From him to whom much has been given

2. He prunes that it may bear more fruit

3. The burdens of others

4. Their own burdens

5. He who shows no mercy

Chapter 11—Be Positive

1. Days

2. Trouble

3. Faith, hope, love

4. Christ

5. Believing in Jesus

Chapter 12—Be Forgiving

1. The unity of the Spirit

2. Forbearance

3. Corban

4. By the Spirit, not by the letter

5. Biting, devouring, and consuming one another

Chapter 13—Be Christlike

1. Humility

2. Death

3. Jesus

4. Let us draw near; let us hold fast

5. Christ in you, the hope of glory

Notes

1. For the full story, see Michael J. Tougias and Casey Sherman, *The Finest Hours: The True Story of the U.S. Coast Guard's Most Daring Sea Rescue* (New York: Scribner, 2009) and Bernie Webber, *Into a Raging Sea: My Life and the Pendleton Rescue*, 2nd ed. (Cape Cod: On Cape Publications, 2015).

2. Crimesider Staff, "Cops Seek Teens Who Allegedly Set Fire to Thirteen-Year-Old Student," *CBS News*, March 5, 2012, accessed November 5, 2018, cbsnews.com/news/cops-seek-teens-who-allegedly-set-fire-to-13-year-old-student/.

3. All passages in this section are quoted from the English Standard Version of the Bible.

PASS IT ON

Have you had a kindness shown?
Pass it on;
'Twas not given for thee alone,
Pass it on;
Let it travel down the years,
Let it wipe another's tears,
Till in heaven the deed appears—
Pass it on.

                —*Henry Burton, 1895*

ABOUT THE AUTHOR

Aubrey Johnson preaches for the Old Hickory Church of Christ in Old Hickory, Tennessee. He is the author of nine books on Christian living and coauthor of *The Best Husband Ever*. Specializing in accentuating the practical benefits of simple New Testament Christianity, Aubrey also conducts church seminars, including Dynamic Deacons, Successful Shepherds, and Get Fit! Church Growth through Church Health. Aubrey is married to the former Lisa Hearn, and they have three sons.